Start Your Business Now

Jeremy Lopez

Start Your Business Now

Published by Dr. Jeremy Lopez

Copyright © 2023

ENDORSEMENTS

Jeremy does an excellent job of giving balanced instruction on how to meditate, and also explaining the benefits that come from having a regular meditation and mindfulness practice. I love how Jeremy is not afraid to learn from and quote those outside the Christian tradition. He is able to explain the ancient concepts simply from a Biblical perspective. – Kari Browning, Director, *The Beautiful Revolution*

You are put on this earth with incredible potential and a divine destiny. This powerful, practical man shows you how to tap into power

Jeremy dives deep into the power of consciousness and shows us that we can create a world where the champion within us can shine and how we can manifest our desires to live a life of fulfillment. A must read! – Greg S. Reid – *Forbes* and *Inc.* top rated Keynote Speaker

I have been privileged to know Jeremy Lopez for many years, as well as sharing the platform with him at a number of conferences. Through this time, I have found him as a man of integrity, commitment, wisdom, and one of the most networked people I have met. Jeremy is an entrepreneur and a leader of leaders. He has amazing insights into leadership competencies and values. He has a passion to ignite this latent potential within individuals and organizations and provide ongoing development and coaching to bring about competitive advantage and success. I would highly recommend him as a

empowered and have strong faith that God has indeed given us these Bible-based Universal and Divine Laws to tap into so that we can live and create an abundant life. – Constance Arnold, M.A., Author, Speaker, Professional Counselor, Host of *The Think, Believe & Manifest Talk Show*

TABLE OF CONTENTS

Introduction

As a success coach, what I've found throughout the past twenty-five years is that everyone has dreams of financial independence. Young and old alike, we're dreamers. I think we're designed that way. What I often hear in coaching sessions is "Jeremy, I have an idea for a business, but where do I begin?" Well, this book, *Start Your Business Now*, is in response to that question.

In the deepest corners of our minds, buried beneath the weight of everyday responsibilities and the pursuit of happiness, lies a common aspiration shared by many: the dream of financial independence. This captivating vision transcends cultural boundaries and economic disparities, resonating with people from all walks of life. It is a dream that often whispers in our ears during moments of solitude, sparking a flicker of hope and igniting the fires of determination.

Financial independence represents more than just wealth and material possessions; it embodies freedom—the freedom to live life on our own terms, unencumbered by the shackles of financial constraints. It is the ability to make choices without being driven solely by financial considerations. Whether it is quitting a job that no longer fulfills us, embarking on a lifelong adventure, or devoting ourselves to causes close to our hearts, financial independence empowers us to shape our destiny.

At its core, the dream of financial independence is an acknowledgment of our desire for autonomy and control over our lives. It is a yearning to break free from the traditional norms that dictate our existence and to chart a course guided by our passions and purpose. The pursuit of financial independence requires discipline, resilience, and strategic planning. It demands that we take a critical look at our relationship with money and reshape our habits and attitudes.

For some, achieving financial independence means amassing significant wealth through investments, entrepreneurship, or career advancements. It entails strategic decisions, calculated risks, and an unwavering focus on long-term goals. These individuals meticulously craft financial plans, diversify their income streams, and constantly seek opportunities for growth.

Others may view financial independence through a lens of simplicity and minimalism. For them, it is about shedding the weight of material possessions and embracing a lifestyle that prioritizes experiences, relationships, and personal well-being over accumulating wealth. They strive to live within their means, practice frugality, and find contentment in the richness of a life unburdened by financial worries.

In the digital age, the dream of financial independence has gained renewed significance. The advent of the internet has ushered in a myriad of opportunities, enabling individuals to explore alternative paths to financial freedom. Online businesses, remote work, and the gig economy have blurred the lines of traditional employment, providing individuals with greater flexibility and control over their earning potential.

Yet, the path to financial independence is not without its challenges. It requires unwavering determination, the ability to navigate uncertainty, and the resilience to overcome setbacks. It demands a keen understanding of personal finance, the discipline to save and invest wisely, and the willingness to make sacrifices in the short term for long-term gain.

Moreover, financial independence is not a one-size-fits-all concept. Each person's journey will be unique, influenced by their circumstances, values, and aspirations. What may represent financial independence for one individual may differ for another. It is essential to recognize and respect these differences, understanding that the path to financial independence is as diverse as the dreams it seeks to fulfill.

Ultimately, the dream of financial independence is a testament to the human spirit's indomitable will to thrive and flourish. It is a reminder that we possess the power to shape our financial destinies and create a life of abundance and freedom. By embracing this dream, we embark on a transformative journey—one that transcends mere monetary goals and ushers us into a world where we are the architects of our own prosperity.

So let us dare to dream of financial independence, for in doing so, we open the door to a future where our dreams become reality and our lives are shaped by the boundless possibilities that lie ahead.

As we embark on the journey towards financial independence, we encounter various milestones and revelations along the way. It is not merely the destination that matters but the lessons learned, the growth experienced, and the transformation that takes place within us.

One of the fundamental realizations we encounter is the importance of mindset. The dream of financial independence requires us to cultivate a mindset of abundance, where we believe that opportunities are abundant and that we are capable of creating our own wealth. It is a shift from a scarcity mindset that limits our potential and hinders our progress. By embracing an abundance mindset, we open ourselves up to possibilities, attract prosperity, and approach challenges with resilience and determination.

In addition to mindset, financial literacy plays a crucial role in our quest for independence. Understanding the principles of personal finance, investing, and wealth management equips us with the knowledge and tools necessary to make informed decisions. Educating ourselves about money empowers us to take control of our financial future, navigate the complexities of the financial world, and avoid pitfalls that can derail our progress.

As we strive towards financial independence, it is essential to remember that the journey is not solely about money. It is about aligning our financial goals with our values, passions, and purpose. True fulfillment comes from living a life that is congruent with our core beliefs and aspirations. Financial independence provides us with the means to pursue our passions, make a positive impact on the world, and cultivate a sense of fulfillment that extends far beyond material wealth.

Along the path to financial independence, we inevitably encounter challenges and setbacks. It is during these moments of adversity that our determination and resilience are tested. However, it is through these challenges that we grow and learn valuable lessons. We discover our inner strength, develop problem-solving skills, and become more adept at navigating the unpredictable nature of life. Every setback becomes an opportunity for growth, and every obstacle serves as a stepping stone towards greater financial independence.

While the dream of financial independence may seem distant and elusive at times, it is crucial to celebrate the small victories along the way. Whether it is paying off debt, reaching a savings milestone, or achieving a financial goal, these accomplishments reaffirm our progress and fuel our motivation to continue moving forward. By acknowledging and appreciating the progress we have made, we cultivate a positive mindset and build momentum towards our ultimate vision of financial independence.

As we near the realization of our dream, it is vital to remember the importance of giving back. Financial independence grants us the ability to make a positive impact on the lives of others and contribute to causes that align with our values. Whether through philanthropy, mentorship, or supporting local communities, we have the opportunity to create a ripple effect of positive change, leaving a lasting legacy that extends far beyond our personal financial achievements.

The dream of financial independence captivates the hearts and minds of individuals across the globe. It represents the pursuit of freedom, autonomy, and fulfillment. As we embark on this transformative journey, let us embrace an abundance mindset, equip ourselves with financial literacy, and align our financial goals with our values. Let us view challenges as opportunities for growth and celebrate our progress along the way. And most importantly, let us use our financial independence as a catalyst for positive change in our lives and the lives of others.

In a world of boundless possibilities and endless opportunities, the decision to start your own business can be a transformative and life-altering choice. It is a step towards autonomy, creativity, and the fulfillment of your entrepreneurial spirit. If you have been contemplating the idea, now is the time to take the leap and embark on the exhilarating journey of entrepreneurship.

Starting your own business allows you to pursue your passions and align your work with your purpose. It is an opportunity to build something meaningful and contribute to the world in a unique and impactful way. Reflect on your interests, skills, and values, and identify a business idea that resonates deeply with you. When your work is driven by passion and purpose, you will find greater fulfillment and motivation to overcome challenges along the way.

Entrepreneurship grants you the freedom to be your own boss and make decisions that shape the direction of your business. You have the autonomy to set your own schedule, choose your clients or customers, and create a work environment that suits your preferences. Embracing this independence allows you to take control of your professional life, breaking free from the constraints of traditional employment.

Starting your own business offers a canvas for your creativity and innovation to flourish. You have the opportunity to develop new products or services, disrupt existing industries, and bring fresh ideas to the market. Entrepreneurship encourages you to think outside the box, experiment with different approaches, and constantly seek improvement and innovation. It is a journey of continuous learning and growth, where your ideas can transform into tangible realities.

Starting a business involves an element of risk and uncertainty. However, it is essential to recognize that calculated risks often lead to the greatest rewards. While fear may be present, embracing it and stepping out of your comfort zone is a necessary part of the entrepreneurial journey. Take the time to assess and manage risks, create a strategic plan, and surround yourself with a support network of mentors, advisors, and like-minded individuals who can guide and inspire you.

Entrepreneurship is a learning process, and setbacks and failures are inevitable. However, these experiences are invaluable opportunities for growth and resilience. Embrace failure as a stepping stone to success, learning from each misstep and adapting your strategies accordingly. The ability to pivot, iterate, and learn from mistakes is a hallmark of successful entrepreneurs. It is through these challenges that you develop the perseverance and determination needed to thrive in the business world.

Entrepreneurship is not a solitary endeavor. Surround yourself with a network of individuals who share your entrepreneurial drive and can offer guidance and support. Attend industry events, join entrepreneurship communities, and seek out mentors who can provide valuable insights and wisdom. Additionally, invest in your own knowledge and skills by attending workshops, taking courses, and staying up-to-date with industry trends. The more you learn and the wider your network becomes, the greater your chances of success.

Often, the biggest obstacle to starting a business is taking that first step. Overcome analysis paralysis by breaking your goals down into smaller, manageable tasks. Begin with a minimum viable product or a pilot project to test the market and gather feedback. Starting small allows you to learn and refine your business model without overwhelming yourself or risking excessive resources. Remember, every great venture starts with a single action.

Starting your own business is an exhilarating and fulfilling journey that offers unparalleled opportunities for personal and professional growth. Embrace your passion, embrace independence, and embrace innovation. Overcome fear and take calculated risks. Learn from failures and adapt your strategies. Seek knowledge and build a strong network of support. But above all, take action and start now.

Delaying your entrepreneurial aspirations can lead to missed opportunities and regrets. The time is ripe, and the world is waiting for your unique contributions. Here are a few reasons why starting your own business now is more advantageous than ever:

In today's digital age, technology has leveled the playing field for entrepreneurs. With the internet, social media, and e-commerce platforms, you have access to a global market right at your fingertips. The power to reach and connect with potential customers has never been easier or more affordable.

The traditional employment landscape is evolving. The gig economy and remote work options have opened up new avenues for entrepreneurial ventures. Many people are embracing flexible work arrangements, and the demand for innovative products and services continues to grow. Seize this opportunity to carve out your niche in an ever-changing market.

Governments and organizations worldwide recognize the vital role entrepreneurship plays in driving economic growth. As a result, there are various support systems and resources available to aspiring entrepreneurs. From grants and funding opportunities to mentorship programs and incubators, these resources can provide you with the guidance and financial backing necessary to kickstart your business.

Starting your own business allows you to create a career that aligns with your values, aspirations, and desired lifestyle. The sense of fulfillment that comes from building something of your own and making a difference in the lives of others is unparalleled. By taking control of your professional destiny, you can experience a level of satisfaction that may elude you in traditional employment.

Being an entrepreneur offers the freedom to adapt and pivot quickly in response to changing market trends and customer needs. Unlike larger corporations, you can make decisions swiftly and implement changes without bureaucratic hurdles. This agility allows you to stay ahead of the curve, outpace competitors, and seize emerging opportunities.

Starting your own business is a transformative journey that pushes you outside your comfort zone and fosters personal growth. As an entrepreneur, you will learn to navigate uncertainty, become a problem solver, develop resilience, and enhance your leadership and decision-making skills. The lessons learned along the way will not only benefit your business but also shape you into a more capable and confident individual.

Entrepreneurship empowers you to leave a lasting legacy and make a meaningful impact. By creating products or services that solve problems, contribute to sustainable practices, or address social issues, you have the opportunity to positively influence the world around you. Your business can become a force for change and inspire others to pursue their dreams.

In conclusion, the time to start your own business is now. Embrace the advantages of our modern era, seize the opportunities available, and embark on a journey of personal and professional fulfillment. Embrace the unknown, learn from failures, and let your entrepreneurial spirit soar. Remember, the world is eagerly waiting for your unique contributions, and the only way to discover what you are truly capable of is by taking that first bold step towards entrepreneurship today.

The Entrepreneurial Mindset

In this chapter, I want to share with you the transformative power of the entrepreneurial mindset and how it can shape your life and pave the way for extraordinary achievements. Whether you aspire to start your own business, pursue a creative endeavor, or simply approach life with a fresh perspective, embracing the entrepreneurial mindset can be the catalyst for unlocking your true potential.

At its core, the entrepreneurial mindset is a unique way of thinking and approaching challenges. It is about seeing opportunities where others see obstacles, embracing calculated risks, and continuously seeking growth and innovation. It is fueled by a deep sense of purpose and an unwavering belief in one's ability to create meaningful change.

One of the key pillars of the entrepreneurial mindset is adopting a growth mindset. This mindset acknowledges that abilities and talents can be developed through dedication, hard work, and a willingness to learn from failures. Instead of fearing setbacks, entrepreneurs view them as valuable learning experiences and stepping stones toward success.

Entrepreneurs possess a keen eye for identifying opportunities that others may overlook. They see gaps in the market, unmet needs, or new ways to solve existing problems. By cultivating curiosity and an open mind, you can train yourself to recognize and capitalize on these opportunities, whether they lie in business, personal endeavors, or social impact.

The entrepreneurial mindset thrives on calculated risk-taking. It acknowledges that with risk comes the potential for great rewards. Entrepreneurs understand that failure is not an endpoint but rather a stepping stone toward success. They embrace failures as learning opportunities, adjust their strategies, and persevere until they achieve their goals.

In the ever-changing landscape of entrepreneurship, resilience and adaptability are indispensable qualities. Entrepreneurs navigate uncertainty, face setbacks, and encounter unforeseen challenges. They learn to adapt quickly, pivot their strategies, and view obstacles as temporary roadblocks rather than insurmountable barriers. Cultivating resilience allows entrepreneurs to bounce back stronger and more determined than ever.

Successful entrepreneurs understand the importance of building a strong network and fostering collaborative relationships. They recognize that no one achieves greatness alone.

By surrounding themselves with like-minded individuals, mentors, and experts in various fields, entrepreneurs gain access to diverse perspectives, valuable insights, and potential partnerships that propel their endeavors forward.

Entrepreneurs possess an unwavering determination and a clear vision of what they want to achieve. They understand that success rarely comes overnight, and they are willing to put in the hard work, dedication, and countless hours required to turn their vision into reality. This persistence, combined with a strong sense of purpose, fuels their drive even during the most challenging times.

The entrepreneurial mindset thrives on a thirst for knowledge and continuous learning. Entrepreneurs are voracious readers, lifelong students, and avid seekers of new information. They stay abreast of industry trends, market shifts, and emerging technologies to ensure their ventures remain relevant and ahead of the curve.

The entrepreneurial mindset is a powerful force that can propel you to new heights in both your personal and professional life. By embracing a growth mindset, seizing opportunities, embracing risk and failure, cultivating resilience, building networks, and staying persistent, you can unlock your full potential and create a lasting impact. Dare to dream big, believe in yourself, and let the entrepreneurial mindset guide you on an extraordinary journey of growth and success.

In this chapter, we will delve deeper into how you can apply the entrepreneurial mindset in practice to maximize its potential and achieve your goals. The entrepreneurial mindset is not just a theoretical concept; it is a way of life that requires action, adaptability, and a relentless pursuit of growth. Let's explore some practical steps you can take to harness the power of this mindset.

The entrepreneurial journey begins with a clear understanding of your purpose. Ask yourself: What drives you? What impact do you want to make? Define your vision and values, and align them with your goals. Establish both short-term and long-term objectives that are specific, measurable, attainable, relevant, and time-bound (SMART). Having a clear direction will serve as your compass and keep you focused on what truly matters.

Entrepreneurs are known for their bias toward action. They don't wait for the perfect moment; they take initiative and make things happen. Embrace a bias toward action by breaking down your goals into smaller, actionable steps. Set deadlines for each step and hold yourself accountable. Remember, progress is more important than perfection. By consistently taking small steps forward, you will build momentum and make significant progress over time.

Entrepreneurs understand that failure is an integral part of the journey to success. Embrace a mindset of experimentation and be open to taking risks. Test your ideas, iterate, and adapt based on feedback and outcomes. If you encounter failure, don't let it discourage you. Instead, view it as an opportunity to learn, adjust your approach, and move forward with newfound knowledge. Failure is not the end; it's a stepping stone on the path to growth and innovation.

The entrepreneurial journey is filled with obstacles and setbacks. To navigate these challenges, cultivate resilience and mental toughness. Cultivate a positive mindset, practice self-care, and surround yourself with a support system that uplifts and motivates you. Seek inspiration from stories of successful entrepreneurs who overcame adversity.

Remember that setbacks are temporary, and your ability to bounce back and keep moving forward will ultimately determine your success.

Never stop learning. In today's fast-paced world, knowledge becomes outdated quickly. Stay ahead by continuously seeking new knowledge and skill development. Read books, attend workshops and conferences, take online courses, and engage in networking events. Seek mentors and experts who can guide you on your journey. Remember, investing in your personal and professional growth is a lifelong commitment that will pay off in the long run.

Surround yourself with like-minded individuals who inspire and challenge you. Seek out mentors, advisors, and peers who can offer guidance and support. Join entrepreneurial communities, both online and offline, where you can exchange ideas, share experiences, and find collaboration opportunities. Building a strong support network will not only provide valuable insights but also foster a sense of camaraderie and accountability.

The entrepreneurial landscape is ever-evolving. Embrace change and be open to new ideas and emerging technologies. Stay curious and explore innovative approaches to problem-solving. Continuously scan the market, identify emerging trends, and adapt your strategies accordingly. Remember, innovation is the lifeblood of entrepreneurship, and those who embrace change will thrive in dynamic environments.

Take time to acknowledge and celebrate your achievements along the way. Celebrating small wins will keep you motivated and reinforce a positive mindset. Reflect on your successes and learn from them. Analyze what worked well, identify the strategies that led to success, and understand the factors that contributed to positive outcomes. Equally important is learning from your achievements. Understand that success can sometimes breed complacency, so it's crucial to remain humble and continue seeking improvement. Use your accomplishments as stepping stones to reach even greater heights.

Entrepreneurship is rarely a solitary journey. Embrace collaboration and seek partnerships that can amplify your impact. Look for opportunities to collaborate with individuals or organizations that share your values and complement your skills. Collaborative efforts can lead to innovative solutions, expanded networks, and shared resources. Foster a spirit of cooperation, be open to different perspectives, and create win-win situations for everyone involved.

In the pursuit of success, it's easy to get caught up in the hustle and lose sight of the present moment. Cultivate gratitude and mindfulness as integral parts of your entrepreneurial mindset. Take time each day to reflect on the things you are grateful for, whether it's personal achievements, supportive relationships, or even the lessons learned from challenges. Practice mindfulness to stay grounded, focused, and in tune with your emotions, allowing you to make more informed decisions and maintain a healthy work-life balance.

As you progress on your entrepreneurial journey and experience the power of the entrepreneurial mindset firsthand, remember to pay it forward. Share your knowledge, mentor aspiring entrepreneurs, and contribute to your community. By supporting others on their paths to success, you not only create a positive impact but also reinforce the entrepreneurial ecosystem that nurtures growth and innovation.

Applying the entrepreneurial mindset is a transformative process that requires intention, action, and continuous self-reflection. By defining your purpose, cultivating a bias toward action, embracing failure, developing resilience, seeking knowledge, building networks, adapting to change, and practicing gratitude, you can harness the true power of the entrepreneurial mindset. Let it guide you toward your goals, fuel your passion, and inspire you to create meaningful impact in the world.

In this chapter, we will explore how the entrepreneurial mindset equips you with the tools to overcome challenges and navigate through the inevitable obstacles you will encounter on your entrepreneurial journey. Building resilience, adapting to change, and maintaining a positive mindset are essential elements in overcoming challenges and turning them into opportunities for growth and success. Let's dive in!

Entrepreneurs thrive on solving problems. Instead of being overwhelmed by challenges, adopt a problem-solving mindset that seeks creative solutions. Break down complex problems into smaller, manageable tasks, and approach them with curiosity and determination. Embrace a mindset that sees challenges as opportunities for innovation and improvement.

Emotional intelligence is crucial for navigating challenges effectively. It involves understanding and managing your own emotions and empathizing with others. Cultivate self-awareness to recognize and regulate your emotions in times of difficulty. Develop empathy to understand the perspectives and emotions of those around you, including team members, customers, and stakeholders. Emotional intelligence will help you navigate conflicts, make better decisions, and build stronger relationships.

Don't be afraid to ask for help when facing challenges. Seek guidance from mentors, advisors, and experienced individuals who can provide valuable insights and advice. Surround yourself with a supportive network of like-minded entrepreneurs who understand the unique challenges you're facing. Collaboration and collective wisdom can often lead to breakthrough solutions and provide a sense of camaraderie during challenging times.

Adopting a growth mindset is vital in overcoming challenges. Believe that your abilities and skills can be developed through effort and perseverance. Embrace challenges as opportunities for learning and growth, even if they initially seem daunting. See setbacks as temporary and view them as valuable lessons that contribute to your personal and professional development. With a growth mindset, you'll be more resilient and determined to find solutions.

Entrepreneurs operate in dynamic environments where change is constant. Embrace change as an inherent part of the entrepreneurial journey. Be flexible and adaptable in your strategies and approaches. Stay attuned to market shifts, customer needs, and emerging trends. Continuously evaluate and adjust your plans to align with new information or circumstances. By being proactive and embracing change, you'll be better prepared to navigate challenges and seize opportunities.

Resilience is the ability to bounce back from setbacks and maintain a positive outlook despite difficulties. Cultivate resilience by reframing challenges as learning experiences and opportunities for growth. Practice self-care to ensure you have the physical and mental energy to face challenges head-on. Build a support system of friends, family, and mentors who can provide encouragement and guidance. Resilience will enable you to persevere through tough times and emerge stronger.

A positive mindset can make a significant difference when facing challenges. Maintaining an optimistic attitude helps you stay motivated, inspire others, and attract positive outcomes. Focus on solutions rather than dwelling on problems. Celebrate small wins and acknowledge progress, no matter how incremental. Surround yourself with positivity and cultivate gratitude for the opportunities and lessons that challenges bring.

Challenges often come with setbacks and failures. Embrace them as learning opportunities and catalysts for growth. Analyze the factors that led to the setback, identify lessons learned, and make adjustments accordingly. View failure as a natural part of the entrepreneurial journey and a stepping stone to success. By learning from setbacks, you'll be better equipped to overcome future challenges and achieve your goals.

Persistence is a key attribute of successful entrepreneurs. When faced with challenges, maintain a steadfast commitment to your goals. Embrace a "never give up" attitude and keep pushing forward, even when the path seems uncertain or difficult. Remember that setbacks are temporary, and success often requires perseverance through obstacles. Stay focused on your vision, and use challenges as opportunities to refine your strategies and find alternative paths to success.

Time management is crucial for navigating challenges effectively. Prioritize your tasks and allocate your time wisely. Identify the most critical and impactful activities that will help you overcome the challenges at hand. Avoid getting overwhelmed by breaking down complex tasks into smaller, manageable steps. Set deadlines and hold yourself accountable. Effective time management ensures that you make progress even in the face of challenges.

Instead of dwelling on the problems, focus on finding solutions. Train your mind to seek opportunities within challenges. Approach problems with a proactive and innovative mindset, exploring different perspectives and possibilities. Collaborate with others to brainstorm ideas and tap into collective wisdom. By maintaining a solution-oriented mindset, you'll be better equipped to overcome challenges and turn them into opportunities for growth and success.

Entrepreneurship inherently involves taking risks, but managing those risks is crucial to navigating challenges successfully. Conduct thorough research, analyze potential outcomes, and develop contingency plans. Assess both the potential rewards and the potential downsides before making decisions. Embrace calculated risks that align with your goals and values while minimizing potential negative impacts. Effective risk management allows you to approach challenges with confidence and preparedness.

In conclusion, challenges are an integral part of the entrepreneurial journey, but with the entrepreneurial mindset, you can overcome them and emerge stronger than before. Embrace a problem-solving mindset, seek support and collaboration, foster a growth mindset, adapt to change, and cultivate resilience and a positive attitude. Learn from setbacks, stay persistent, manage your time effectively, and maintain a solution-oriented approach. With these strategies, you'll be equipped to face any challenge and turn it into an opportunity for growth and success on your entrepreneurial path. Wishing you resilience, determination, and breakthroughs on your entrepreneurial journey.

Finding Your Passion

By recognizing your passion, you have taken the first step towards transforming your life. Now, it's time to embark on an exciting journey of turning that passion into a successful business. In this chapter, we will explore the key steps and considerations that will help you channel your passion into a sustainable venture. So, let's dive in and unleash your entrepreneurial spirit!

To build a business around your passion, you must clearly define what it is that truly drives you. Take some time to reflect on your interests, talents, and the activities that bring you joy. Think about the skills you possess and the knowledge you have acquired. Identify the niche within your passion that resonates with you the most. By pinpointing your passion, you will lay a solid foundation for your future business.

Now that you have identified your passion, it's essential to conduct thorough market research. Understand your target audience and analyze the demand for products or services related to your passion. Identify your competitors, study their offerings, and find ways to differentiate yourself. This research will provide valuable insights into the feasibility and potential profitability of your business.

To stand out from the competition, you need to develop a unique value proposition. Consider how your business can solve a problem, fulfill a need, or offer something different. Identify the core benefits your customers will receive from your products or services. Craft a compelling value proposition that clearly communicates why customers should choose your business over others. Your unique value proposition will be the cornerstone of your marketing and branding efforts.

A well-structured business plan is crucial for success. It serves as a roadmap, guiding you through the initial stages and helping you make informed decisions. Outline your business goals, strategies, and financial projections. Define your target market, pricing strategy, and marketing tactics. Set realistic milestones and establish a timeline for achieving them. A solid business plan will not only keep you focused but also serve as a vital tool when seeking financing or partnerships.

While your passion provides the foundation, building a business requires a diverse skill set. Identify the areas where you lack expertise and take steps to acquire or develop those skills. It could involve attending workshops, taking online courses, or finding a mentor who can guide you along the way. Building business acumen will enhance your ability to manage finances, marketing, operations, and other critical aspects of entrepreneurship.

Surrounding yourself with supportive individuals who share your passion and entrepreneurial mindset is crucial. Attend industry events, join professional networks, and engage with like-minded individuals. Seek mentorship from experienced entrepreneurs who can offer valuable advice and insights. A strong network will provide opportunities for collaboration, learning, and growth.

When turning your passion into a business, it's wise to start small and test your ideas before fully committing. Create a minimal viable product or offer pilot services to gather feedback and validate your business concept. This approach allows you to iterate and refine your offerings based on real-world experiences. Use customer feedback to fine-tune your business model, and don't be afraid to pivot if necessary.

Effective marketing and branding are essential for attracting customers. Develop a compelling brand identity that reflects your passion, values, and unique selling proposition. Leverage social media platforms, content marketing, and other digital channels to reach your target audience. Engage with your customers, build relationships, and provide value through your content. Consistently communicate your brand message and create an emotional connection with your audience.

Embrace these challenges as learning experiences and opportunities to refine your business. Stay adaptable and open to change, as the market and customer needs may evolve over time. Be proactive in seeking feedback, analyzing market trends, and making necessary adjustments to stay ahead of the curve.

Running a business can be overwhelming at times, and it's important to seek support when needed. Surround yourself with a team of talented individuals who share your passion and complement your skills. Delegate tasks to focus on what you do best and consider outsourcing certain functions if necessary. Additionally, explore collaborations and partnerships that can expand your reach and bring new opportunities to your business.

Financial management is critical for the success of your business. Keep a close eye on your finances, regularly review your income and expenses, and maintain accurate records. Create a budget and monitor cash flow to ensure sustainability. If you require additional funding to scale your business, explore different options such as small business loans, grants, or crowdfunding. Present your business plan and financial projections confidently to potential investors or lenders.

As your business grows, it's crucial to stay connected to your passion. Remember why you started this journey and let your enthusiasm shine through. Continually seek ways to evolve your products or services, staying attuned to market trends and customer feedback. Stay curious and embrace lifelong learning to stay ahead in your industry. By infusing your passion into every aspect of your business, you will inspire others and create a lasting impact.

Turning your passion into a thriving business requires dedication, perseverance, and a strategic approach. By following these steps and staying true to your passion, you can create a business that aligns with your values and brings you joy. Remember, success may not come overnight, but with a solid plan, continuous learning, and a customer-centric mindset, you can transform your passion into a rewarding and sustainable entrepreneurial venture. Embrace the challenges, celebrate the victories, and enjoy the fulfilling journey of building a business around what you love.

In the hustle and bustle of everyday life, it's easy to get caught up in the routine and lose sight of what truly drives us. However, finding your passion is not just a luxury; it is a fundamental aspect of living a fulfilling and purposeful life. In this chapter, we will explore the importance of discovering your passion and how it can positively impact every aspect of your life.

Your passion is like a flame that burns deep within you. It is the spark that ignites your enthusiasm, fuels your motivation, and brings joy to your daily activities. When you discover and pursue your passion, you unlock a source of intrinsic motivation that propels you forward, even in the face of challenges. It gives you a sense of purpose and fulfillment, making each day more meaningful.

Each of us possesses a unique set of talents, skills, and gifts. However, it is through the exploration of our passions that we truly uncover and harness these abilities. When you engage in activities that align with your passion, you tap into your natural strengths and abilities, allowing you to excel and make a significant impact in those areas. Your passion becomes a conduit for self-expression and personal growth, leading to a sense of accomplishment and self-confidence.

Numerous studies have shown that pursuing your passion is directly linked to increased well-being and happiness. Engaging in activities that you are passionate about releases endorphins, reduces stress levels, and boosts your overall mood. It provides a sense of purpose, fulfillment, and satisfaction that can positively impact your mental, emotional, and even physical health.

Your passion becomes a source of inner joy and contentment, making each day more vibrant and meaningful.

Finding your passion is often intertwined with uncovering your life's purpose. When you engage in activities that align with your passion, you are living authentically and in alignment with your core values. Your passion serves as a compass, guiding you towards a greater sense of purpose and meaning in life. It allows you to make choices that align with your true self, leading to a more fulfilled and purpose-driven existence.

Passion is a catalyst for continuous learning and personal growth. When you are passionate about something, you are naturally inclined to seek knowledge, improve your skills, and explore new possibilities within that realm. It drives you to constantly challenge yourself, step out of your comfort zone, and acquire new experiences. By pursuing your passion, you embark on a lifelong journey of self-discovery, learning, and growth.

Your passion has the power to inspire and impact those around you. When you are engaged in activities that you are truly passionate about, your enthusiasm becomes contagious. It radiates through your words, actions, and interactions, inspiring others to pursue their own passions and live authentically. By living as an example, you have the opportunity to positively influence and contribute to the lives of others.

Discovering and pursuing your passion allows you to leave a lasting legacy. When you align your actions with your passion, you make a meaningful contribution to the world. Whether it is through creating art, solving problems, helping others, or driving innovation, your passion becomes a vehicle for making a positive impact and leaving a mark on society. Your legacy becomes a testament to a life well-lived and a passion fully embraced.

Finding your passion is not a luxury or a mere indulgence; it is a fundamental aspect of living a fulfilling and purposeful life. It fuels your motivation, ignites your inner fire, and propels you towards personal growth and happiness. By embracing your passion, you tap into your unique talents, unleash your potential, and find meaning in your daily pursuits.

Your passion is not just for your own benefit. It has the power to inspire and impact others, creating a ripple effect of positivity and motivation. When you live authentically and pursue your passion, you become a source of inspiration for those around you, encouraging them to discover and embrace their own passions.

Furthermore, finding your passion allows you to leave a lasting legacy. By aligning your actions with your passion, you make a meaningful contribution to the world. Whether it is through your work, creativity, or acts of service, your passion becomes a vehicle for making a positive impact and leaving a mark on society. Your legacy becomes a testament to a life well-lived and a passion fully embraced.

In the pursuit of your passion, you embark on a journey of continuous learning and growth. You push the boundaries of your comfort zone, acquire new skills and knowledge, and embrace new experiences. This journey of self-discovery not only expands your horizons but also opens doors to new opportunities and possibilities.

Ultimately, finding your passion is about living a life that is true to yourself. It is about honoring your authentic desires and values, and creating a life that brings you joy, fulfillment, and a sense of purpose. Your passion becomes the compass that guides your choices, propelling you towards a life that is meaningful and aligned with your true self.

So, take the time to explore, reflect, and discover what truly ignites your soul. Embrace your passions, for they hold the key to a life filled with purpose, happiness, and personal fulfillment. Remember that your passion is unique to you, and it is never too late to embark on the journey of uncovering and pursuing it. Embrace the journey, follow your heart, and let your passion light the way towards a life that truly resonates with your deepest desires and aspirations.

Understanding Your Audience

In the vast and competitive landscape of business, success hinges on the ability to connect with the right people – your target audience. Understanding who your target audience is and catering to their needs and preferences is essential for building a thriving business. In this chapter, we will delve into the importance of finding your target audience and explore strategies to identify and engage with them effectively.

Before embarking on any business venture, it is crucial to define your target audience. Your target audience is the specific group of people who are most likely to be interested in your products or services. Identifying your target audience allows you to focus your efforts and resources where they will yield the highest returns.

To define your target audience, consider the following factors:

Demographics: Age, gender, location, income level, occupation, and education.

Psychographics: Interests, values, attitudes, lifestyles, and behavior patterns.

The problems your audience faces and how your products or services can solve them.

By gathering data and analyzing these factors, you can create a detailed profile of your ideal customer, enabling you to tailor your marketing and communication strategies accordingly.

Once you have identified your target audience, you can refine your marketing efforts to effectively reach and engage with them.

Tailoring your marketing strategy ensures that your message resonates with your intended audience, increasing the chances of conversions and customer loyalty.

Here are some strategies to consider:

Clearly communicate the unique benefits your products or services offer to address the specific needs and challenges of your target audience.

Determine the platforms and channels your target audience uses most frequently and establish a presence there. It could be social media platforms, industry-specific websites, or offline channels like events or trade shows.

Create content that speaks directly to your target audience. Address their pain points, provide solutions, and showcase how your offerings can enhance their lives or businesses.

Continuously monitor and analyze data to gain insights into your audience's behavior, preferences, and purchasing patterns. This information can help refine your marketing campaigns and improve customer targeting.

Finding your target audience is not just about attracting new customers; it is also about building lasting relationships. By understanding your audience's needs, preferences, and pain points, you can tailor your products, services, and customer experience to meet and exceed their expectations.

Consider these strategies for building stronger customer relationships: Customize your interactions, offers, and communications to make customers feel valued and understood. Use their names, send personalized recommendations, and provide relevant content.

Encourage dialogue with your target audience through social media, surveys, and feedback forms. Actively listen to their opinions, address concerns promptly, and incorporate their suggestions into your business processes.

Deliver exceptional customer service experiences that leave a lasting positive impression. Train your team to be attentive, empathetic, and responsive, ensuring customer satisfaction at every touchpoint.

Implement loyalty programs or rewards systems that incentivize repeat purchases and customer referrals. Offer exclusive benefits and discounts to strengthen customer loyalty and encourage advocacy.

In the vast sea of potential customers, finding your target audience is the compass that guides your business toward success. By understanding who your target audience is, tailoring your marketing efforts, and building stronger customer relationships, you position your business for growth, profitability, and long-term sustainability.

Remember, finding your target audience is an ongoing process. As markets evolve and customer preferences change, stay attuned to these shifts and adapt your strategies accordingly. Embrace the power of connecting with the right audience, and you will unlock a world of opportunities for your business.

In today's digital age, where information and products are readily available at the click of a button, finding your target audience is more critical than ever. With countless options and competitors vying for attention, it is essential to stand out and connect with the right people who genuinely resonate with your brand.

When you identify and engage with your target audience effectively, you have the opportunity to cultivate brand advocates. These are loyal customers who not only love your products or services but also actively promote your brand to others. They become your greatest asset in expanding your reach and influence.

By focusing your efforts on your target audience, you can provide them with an exceptional customer experience, exceed their expectations, and create a community around your brand. Satisfied customers will spread positive word-of-mouth, recommend your offerings to friends and colleagues, and even defend your brand during challenging times. This organic promotion not only saves you marketing costs but also builds trust and credibility, attracting more like-minded individuals to your business.

Understanding your target audience allows you to optimize your resources effectively. Every business has limited time, energy, and financial resources, and it's crucial to allocate them in the most efficient way possible.

By defining your target audience, you can focus your marketing efforts on the channels and platforms that are most relevant to them. For example, if your target audience consists of young professionals, investing in social media platforms like Instagram and LinkedIn may yield better results than traditional print advertisements.

Moreover, knowing your target audience's preferences and interests enables you to tailor your content, messages, and campaigns to resonate with them effectively. This targeted approach enhances the effectiveness of your marketing efforts and ensures that you are investing your resources where they will have the highest impact.

Your target audience serves as a valuable source of insights for developing new products and improving existing ones. By understanding their needs, pain points, and desires, you can innovate and create offerings that directly address their specific requirements.

Regularly engaging with your target audience through surveys, focus groups, or online communities can provide you with invaluable feedback. They can offer suggestions, identify areas for improvement, and even inspire new ideas. By incorporating their feedback into your product development process, you increase the likelihood of creating solutions that resonate with your target audience and meet their expectations.

Additionally, your target audience can also guide your pricing strategies. Understanding their willingness to pay and perceived value can help you set prices that are both competitive and profitable. This knowledge allows you to strike the right balance between affordability and profitability, maximizing your revenue potential.

Finding your target audience is a fundamental step in building a successful business. By defining your target audience, tailoring your marketing efforts, and nurturing strong relationships, you can unlock numerous benefits such as increased brand advocacy, efficient resource allocation, and improved product development.

Remember that finding your target audience is an ongoing process. As markets and consumer behaviors evolve, continuously evaluate and refine your understanding of your target audience. Stay attuned to their changing needs, preferences, and trends, and adapt your strategies accordingly. By doing so, you will position your business for long-term growth, sustainability, and continued success.

Finding your target audience enables you to communicate your brand message effectively. When you understand who your audience is, you can speak their language, address their specific pain points, and highlight the benefits of your products or services that resonate with them.

By tailoring your communication and messaging to your target audience, you can capture their attention and create a meaningful connection. Your marketing materials, website content, social media posts, and advertisements can be crafted to speak directly to their needs, aspirations, and values. This personalized approach makes your brand more relatable, increases engagement, and enhances the likelihood of converting leads into loyal customers.

Furthermore, understanding your target audience allows you to choose the most effective marketing channels and platforms for reaching them. Whether it's through social media, email marketing, content marketing, or offline advertising, you can focus your efforts on the channels that have the highest potential for reaching and engaging with your target audience.

Identifying and understanding your target audience gives you a competitive advantage in the marketplace. By focusing on a specific group of people, you can differentiate your brand from competitors and position yourself as the go-to solution provider for their needs.

While your competitors may be trying to appeal to a broad range of customers, your targeted approach allows you to cater to your audience's unique requirements more effectively. This specialized focus enables you to tailor your offerings, marketing strategies, and customer experience to match the specific desires and preferences of your target audience.

Moreover, by continuously engaging with your target audience and staying attuned to their evolving needs, you can stay one step ahead of your competitors. You can identify emerging trends, anticipate changes in consumer behavior, and proactively adjust your strategies to maintain your relevance and competitive edge.

Finding your target audience is a cornerstone of business success. It empowers you to communicate effectively, allocate resources efficiently, build strong customer relationships, and gain a competitive advantage. By investing time and effort in understanding and connecting with your target audience, you can position your business for long-term growth, profitability, and sustainability.

Remember that your target audience is not a static entity. Consumer preferences, behaviors, and demographics may evolve over time. Stay proactive in monitoring and adapting to these changes, and regularly reassess your understanding of your target audience to ensure that your strategies remain relevant and effective. By doing so, you will continue to engage and serve your target audience successfully, leading to ongoing business success.

One of the most significant benefits of finding your target audience is the ability to generate meaningful leads and conversions. When you focus your marketing efforts on the right people, you attract individuals who are more likely to be interested in what you have to offer. This targeted approach increases the quality of leads you generate and improves your conversion rates.

By understanding your target audience's needs, pain points, and motivations, you can create compelling marketing campaigns that speak directly to them. Your messaging and offers will resonate with their desires, making them more likely to take action and become customers. This alignment between your offerings and their needs increases the likelihood of conversions, resulting in a higher return on investment (ROI) for your marketing efforts.

Furthermore, by tailoring your marketing messages to your target audience's preferences and interests, you can create personalized experiences that engage and captivate them. Personalization fosters a sense of connection and trust, making potential customers more inclined to choose your brand over competitors.

In a rapidly evolving business landscape, adaptability is crucial for long-term success. By identifying and understanding your target audience, you position your business to adapt to changes and seize new opportunities for growth.

As you engage with your target audience, you gain insights into their evolving needs, preferences, and market trends. This knowledge enables you to innovate and evolve your products or services to meet their changing demands. By staying ahead of the curve, you can maintain your relevance, attract new customers, and retain existing ones.

Moreover, understanding your target audience helps you identify untapped market segments or niche opportunities. It allows you to explore new customer groups that align with your brand and offerings. By expanding your reach and attracting additional target audiences, you diversify your customer base and reduce the risks associated with relying on a single market segment.

Finding your target audience is an indispensable component of achieving business success. It enables you to generate meaningful leads, increase conversions, and foster customer loyalty. By understanding your audience's needs, tailoring your marketing efforts, and remaining adaptable, you position your business to thrive in an ever-changing marketplace.

Remember, finding your target audience is an ongoing process. Regularly review and update your audience profiles as market dynamics and consumer behaviors evolve. Embrace feedback and insights from your customers, use data analytics to refine your strategies, and continuously strive to connect with your target audience in meaningful and relevant ways. By doing so, you will unlock the full potential of your business and build a foundation for long-term growth and prosperity.

Crafting a Winning Business Plan

In the vast landscape of entrepreneurship, a well-crafted and meticulously executed business plan serves as the compass that guides your journey towards success. A winning business plan encapsulates your vision, goals, strategies, and financial projections in a cohesive roadmap that paves the way for growth and prosperity. This chapter delves into the significance of having a winning business plan, outlining its key benefits and offering insights on how to create one.

A winning business plan acts as a blueprint for your entrepreneurial endeavors. It forces you to articulate your vision, define your objectives, and clarify the steps required to achieve them. By meticulously documenting your business idea, market analysis, target audience, and competitive advantage, you gain a deeper understanding of your own venture. This clarity helps you stay focused, make informed decisions, and align your resources towards achieving your goals.

When it comes to securing external financing, a winning business plan is your best ally. Investors and lenders are naturally drawn to entrepreneurs who exhibit a thorough understanding of their market, competition, and growth potential. A well-documented plan demonstrates your commitment, expertise, and ability to mitigate risks. It showcases your financial projections, including revenue streams, cost structures, and return on investment, which helps instill confidence in potential investors. A winning business plan acts as a powerful tool to attract funding, forge strategic partnerships, and bring your entrepreneurial dreams to fruition.

Running a successful business requires making countless decisions on a daily basis. A winning business plan empowers you with a framework to make informed choices. It enables you to evaluate the feasibility of new opportunities, assess risks, and weigh the potential benefits against the costs involved. With a comprehensive plan in hand, you can make decisions that align with your long-term vision and strategic goals, thereby increasing the likelihood of achieving sustainable success.

By creating a winning business plan, you delve deep into the operational aspects of your venture. This process compels you to analyze workflows, streamline processes, and identify potential bottlenecks. Through this critical examination, you can identify areas where resources can be optimized, costs can be reduced, and efficiency can be improved. By having a clear roadmap and defined operational strategies, you can enhance productivity, minimize waste, and maximize profits.

A winning business plan not only focuses on the present but also envisions the future growth and expansion of your venture. It allows you to set realistic milestones and develop strategies to achieve them. By forecasting financial projections and market trends, you can identify potential opportunities and challenges that lie ahead. This foresight helps you adapt your business model, capitalize on emerging trends, and position your company for long-term success.

In the ever-changing landscape of entrepreneurship, a winning business plan is your anchor, providing stability, focus, and direction. It not only serves as a valuable tool to attract investors and secure funding but also acts as a roadmap that guides your decision-making, promotes operational efficiency, and enables strategic growth. By investing time and effort into crafting a comprehensive business plan, you lay the foundation for a successful and thriving enterprise. Embrace the power of planning, and let your winning business plan become your ultimate ally in the pursuit of entrepreneurial excellence.

A winning business plan establishes clear benchmarks and performance indicators that allow you to track progress and measure success. By setting specific goals and timelines, you create a framework for accountability. Regularly reviewing and updating your business plan enables you to monitor key metrics, identify areas for improvement, and make necessary adjustments to stay on track. The ability to measure your performance against predetermined targets helps you stay focused and motivated, ensuring that you are consistently moving closer to your overarching objectives.

Resource management is a critical aspect of running a successful business. With a winning business plan, you gain a comprehensive understanding of the resources required to execute your strategies effectively. Whether it's financial resources, human capital, technology, or infrastructure, your business plan helps you allocate resources in a strategic and cost-effective manner. It helps you prioritize investments, identify potential gaps, and ensure that resources are utilized efficiently to drive growth and profitability.

In today's competitive business landscape, having a winning business plan sets you apart from the crowd. It showcases your professionalism, strategic thinking, and attention to detail. A well-crafted plan demonstrates that you have conducted thorough market research, analyzed your competition, and developed unique value propositions. This comprehensive understanding of your market positioning and competitive advantage helps you differentiate your business and attract customers, partners, and talented individuals who believe in your vision.

Starting a business inherently involves risks, but a winning business plan helps you identify, assess, and mitigate those risks. By conducting a SWOT analysis (Strengths, Weaknesses, Opportunities, and Threats), you gain valuable insights into potential obstacles and challenges. This enables you to develop contingency plans and risk management strategies to minimize their impact on your business. By proactively addressing risks in your business plan, you enhance your ability to navigate uncertainties and adapt to changing market conditions.

A winning business plan serves as a powerful communication tool, both internally and externally. Internally, it aligns your team members around a shared vision, goals, and strategies. It provides a common understanding of the direction in which your business is headed, fostering collaboration and teamwork. Externally, your business plan communicates your value proposition to stakeholders, partners, and customers. It conveys your credibility, professionalism, and commitment to delivering value, thus building trust and enhancing your brand reputation.

A winning business plan is not a static document but a dynamic tool that evolves with your business. It serves as a compass, guiding you through the challenges and opportunities that lie ahead. By providing clarity, attracting investors, facilitating decision-making, promoting efficiency, guiding growth, and enhancing accountability, a well-crafted business plan becomes an indispensable asset in your entrepreneurial journey. Embrace the power of planning, and let your winning business plan become the cornerstone of your success story.

In today's fast-paced and ever-evolving business landscape, adaptability and agility are crucial for survival. A winning business plan empowers you to anticipate market changes, technological advancements, and shifting consumer demands. By regularly reviewing and updating your plan, you can adapt your strategies, explore new opportunities, and pivot when necessary. This flexibility allows you to stay ahead of the curve, capitalize on emerging trends, and maintain a competitive edge.

A winning business plan serves as a foundation for your marketing and sales efforts. It helps you define your target audience, understand their needs, and develop strategies to reach and engage them effectively. With a well-defined marketing and sales plan in place, you can allocate resources to the most impactful channels, craft compelling messaging, and create a strong brand presence. Your business plan ensures that your marketing and sales efforts are aligned with your overall business objectives, maximizing your chances of attracting and retaining customers.

A comprehensive and well-structured business plan instills confidence in your team members, stakeholders, and partners. It showcases your leadership skills, strategic thinking, and ability to navigate complexities. By communicating your vision, goals, and strategies, you inspire trust and motivate others to join you on your entrepreneurial journey. A winning business plan demonstrates your commitment to success and your ability to navigate challenges with resilience and determination.

As your business evolves and grows, a winning business plan becomes a valuable reference point for decision-making. It provides a historical record of your initial intentions, milestones achieved, and lessons learned. By reflecting on your business plan, you can evaluate your progress, identify areas for improvement, and celebrate your achievements. Additionally, it can be a useful tool when seeking feedback, advice, or mentorship from experienced entrepreneurs or industry experts.

A winning business plan is not only essential for starting a business but also for planning its long-term sustainability. It lays the groundwork for succession planning and exit strategies, allowing you to envision the future of your business beyond your own involvement. By including provisions for leadership transitions, ownership transfers, or potential exits, you ensure a smooth transition and maximize the value of your business when the time comes.

A winning business plan is more than just a document; it is a dynamic roadmap that guides your entrepreneurial journey. It provides clarity, attracts funding, facilitates decision-making, promotes efficiency, and guides growth. Moreover, it fosters adaptability, inspires confidence, and serves as a reference point for your business's evolution. Embrace the importance of having a winning business plan, and let it be your guiding compass to navigate the challenges and seize the opportunities that lie ahead. Remember, a well-crafted plan sets the stage for a successful and fulfilling entrepreneurial endeavor.

A winning business plan instills discipline and accountability within your organization. It sets clear goals, timelines, and targets that everyone can align with and work towards. By regularly reviewing and assessing progress against the plan, you create a culture of accountability where team members take ownership of their responsibilities. This discipline ensures that everyone remains focused on the strategic objectives and actively contributes to the overall success of the business.

Resource allocation is a critical aspect of running a successful business. A winning business plan helps you allocate resources strategically and efficiently. By outlining the financial requirements, staffing needs, and operational expenses, you can optimize the allocation of resources to maximize productivity and minimize waste. This proactive approach to resource management allows you to make informed decisions on where to invest, cut costs, or reallocate assets to areas that have the highest impact on your business objectives.

A winning business plan serves as a foundation for continuous improvement and learning. It encourages you to regularly evaluate and reassess your strategies, processes, and outcomes. By analyzing market trends, customer feedback, and performance metrics, you can identify areas for improvement and implement necessary adjustments. This iterative approach to business management enables you to adapt to changing circumstances, stay ahead of the competition, and consistently deliver value to your customers.

Businesses operate in an environment of uncertainty and risk. A winning business plan helps you identify potential risks and develop risk management strategies to mitigate their impact. By conducting thorough market research, competitor analysis, and scenario planning, you can proactively address risks and devise contingency plans. This risk management approach minimizes the likelihood of negative surprises and equips you with the ability to navigate unforeseen challenges with resilience and agility.

Ultimately, a winning business plan sets the foundation for long-term sustainability and success. It enables you to align your short-term actions with your long-term vision and goals. By considering factors such as market trends, industry dynamics, and customer preferences, you can develop strategies that position your business for longevity. A well-crafted plan also ensures that you remain focused on your core values, purpose, and unique value proposition, which are instrumental in building a strong and sustainable brand over time.

Having a winning business plan is not a luxury; it is a necessity for any aspiring entrepreneur or business owner. It provides clarity, accountability, and discipline while guiding your decision-making, resource allocation, and risk management efforts. A well-structured plan supports growth, continuous improvement, and long-term sustainability. Embrace the importance of a winning business plan and make it an integral part of your entrepreneurial journey, as it will be the compass that keeps you on the path to success amidst the challenges and uncertainties of the business world.

A winning business plan instills confidence in you as an entrepreneur and in your team members. It provides a clear roadmap and strategy to follow, giving you a sense of direction and purpose. This confidence translates into resilience when facing obstacles or setbacks. With a solid plan in place, you are better equipped to overcome challenges, adapt to unforeseen circumstances, and persevere in the face of adversity. The knowledge that you have a well-thought-out plan gives you the confidence to navigate through difficult times and emerge stronger.

A winning business plan serves as a communication tool that aligns your team members, stakeholders, and partners. It provides a common understanding of the business objectives, strategies, and expectations. By sharing your plan with others, you foster a sense of unity and collaboration. It enables effective communication by clearly articulating the purpose, values, and goals of your business. When everyone is aligned and working towards the same vision, the collective effort becomes more focused, efficient, and productive.

A winning business plan helps you understand your target audience and develop strategies to meet their needs effectively. By conducting market research and analysis, you gain valuable insights into customer preferences, pain points, and buying behaviors. This knowledge allows you to tailor your products or services, marketing messages, and customer experiences to create a strong connection with your target market. A well-crafted plan ensures that you consistently deliver value and build long-lasting relationships with your customers, leading to customer loyalty and positive word-of-mouth.

A winning business plan takes into account the potential for scalability and expansion. It outlines strategies to grow your business, enter new markets, or introduce new products and services. By considering factors such as market demand, operational capabilities, and financial projections, you can identify opportunities for growth and develop a roadmap to pursue them. This proactive approach to planning for expansion sets the stage for sustainable growth and maximizes the potential of your business in the long run.

When you present a winning business plan to investors, lenders, or potential partners, it positions you as a serious and dedicated entrepreneur. It demonstrates your commitment to success, your professionalism, and your ability to plan for the future. A well-prepared plan showcases your expertise, market knowledge, and strategic thinking, instilling confidence in others to invest in or collaborate with your venture. It sets you apart from others who may not have a clear roadmap or a comprehensive understanding of their business.

Having a winning business plan is a fundamental element of building a successful business. It provides clarity, confidence, and resilience while aligning your team, attracting stakeholders, and guiding decision-making. A well-crafted plan supports effective communication, customer relationships, and scalability. It positions you as a serious entrepreneur and sets the foundation for long-term success. Embrace the importance of a winning business plan and make it an integral part of your entrepreneurial journey, as it will serve as your compass to navigate the challenges, capitalize on opportunities, and achieve your business aspirations.

Funding Your Venture

It may not seem like it now, but there are people in the world who will believe in you and believe in your vision. You just have to know where to look. As you embark on your journey of bringing your vision to life, it's essential to remember that you are not alone. Throughout history, countless visionaries have encountered skeptics, doubters, and naysayers. But there is a beautiful truth that lies within the vast tapestry of humanity – there are others who will believe in your vision.

When you dare to dream big and chase after your vision, it can often feel like an isolating experience. The weight of doubt and uncertainty may attempt to drag you down. But it is precisely during these moments that you must seek out your visionary tribe, a community of like-minded individuals who share your passion and believe in what you stand for.

Your visionary tribe consists of people who recognize the potential and value in your ideas. They are individuals who understand that true progress often emerges from unconventional thinking. They see beyond the limitations imposed by the status quo, envisioning a future that is different and better.

To find your tribe, start by immersing yourself in communities, both physical and virtual, that align with your interests and goals. Attend conferences, join forums, engage in networking events, and seek out mentorship from those who have already walked a similar path. Share your vision, be open to feedback, and connect with those who resonate with your ideas.

Within your visionary tribe, you will encounter individuals who possess diverse skills, experiences, and perspectives. Some may be artists, engineers, entrepreneurs, or activists. Each person brings a unique contribution to the collective tapestry of your vision.

Nurture these relationships and cultivate a spirit of collaboration. By embracing the strengths of others, you can build a network that not only supports your vision but propels it forward. Remember, great visions are rarely achieved alone – they are the culmination of collective effort.

Your visionary tribe may consist of people who share a common goal but approach it from various angles. Embrace these differences as opportunities for growth and innovation. Diverse perspectives challenge your assumptions, helping you refine and strengthen your vision.

Encourage open dialogue and foster an environment where everyone feels heard and valued. Acknowledge that disagreements and healthy debates are essential for progress. By creating a safe space for diverse opinions, you will foster an atmosphere of mutual respect and intellectual growth.

As your vision gains momentum and begins to materialize, your visionary tribe will extend beyond your immediate circle. The ripples of your influence will reach new horizons, attracting like-minded individuals who resonate with your purpose.

Embrace this expanding tribe with open arms. Offer guidance, mentorship, and encouragement to those who are just starting their journey. By paying it forward, you not only create a lasting impact but also inspire others to believe in their own visions.

Building a visionary tribe is not a one-time effort; it is an ongoing process. Nurturing these relationships requires time, dedication, and genuine care. As your vision evolves, so will the needs and aspirations of your tribe members.

Stay connected, provide support, and collaborate on new ventures. Engage in regular communication through newsletters, online platforms, or even in-person meetups. Celebrate milestones together, learn from shared experiences, and adapt your vision as you collectively navigate the ever-changing landscape.

In the vast expanse of this world, there are people waiting to join you on your visionary journey. They are ready to believe in your vision, contribute their unique talents, and help you overcome the obstacles that lie ahead.

So, my dear dreamer, have faith and trust in the power of connection and the unwavering support of your visionary tribe. Surround yourself with those who lift you up, challenge you to grow, and inspire you to reach greater heights.

In the face of adversity, when doubt creeps in, remember that you are not alone. Your tribe stands by your side, bolstering your confidence, and reminding you of the impact your vision can make.

Together, you can weather the storms, overcome obstacles, and turn setbacks into stepping stones. Your tribe believes in your potential, your ideas, and the positive change you seek to bring into the world.

As you navigate the twists and turns of your journey, don't be discouraged by the occasional setback or momentary doubt. Remember that every great visionary faced challenges, but it was their unwavering belief and the unwavering support of their tribe that propelled them forward.

Your vision has the potential to shape the world, to ignite passion and spark innovation. It is a beacon of hope, a catalyst for transformation, and a testament to the power of human imagination.

So, my dear dreamer, never lose sight of the fact that there are others who will believe in your vision. Seek them out, nurture those relationships, and embrace the collective strength that comes from working together towards a common purpose.

Embrace your visionary tribe, for within their unwavering support lies the fuel to ignite your dreams and turn them into reality. The journey may be challenging, but remember that you are not alone. You have a tribe of believers standing beside you, ready to champion your vision and help you bring it to life.

Believe in yourself, trust in your vision, and let your tribe be the wind beneath your wings as you soar towards a brighter future. Together, you have the power to make a lasting impact and leave a remarkable legacy.

Embrace the knowledge that there are others who will believe in your vision, and let their unwavering support be the foundation upon which you build your dreams.

Starting a new business venture requires adequate financial resources to turn your vision into reality. In this chapter, we will explore various funding options available to entrepreneurs like yourself. Each option has its own advantages and considerations, so it's important to carefully evaluate which one suits your specific business needs and goals.

Self-Funding:

Self-funding, also known as bootstrapping, involves using your personal savings, assets, or credit to finance your business. While this method allows you to maintain full control over your venture, it does require a significant personal investment. Considerations for self-funding include:

Savings: Utilize your personal savings or liquidate investments to provide initial capital.

Credit Cards: Use credit cards for short-term financing, but be mindful of high interest rates.

Home Equity: Tap into the equity of your property through loans or lines of credit.

Friends and Family:

Approaching friends and family for financial support can be an effective way to secure initial funding. However, it's crucial to approach these relationships with care and establish clear expectations and repayment terms. Consider the following when seeking funding from friends and family:

Transparency: Clearly communicate your business plan, risks involved, and potential returns.

Legal Documentation: Create a written agreement specifying the terms of the investment, such as equity shares or repayment plans.

Professionalism: Treat the arrangement as you would with any other investor to maintain a strong personal and professional relationship.

Business Loans:

Obtaining a business loan from a financial institution can provide you with the necessary capital to start or expand your venture. Here are a few key factors to consider when seeking a business loan:

Research: Explore different loan options and compare interest rates, repayment terms, and collateral requirements.

Business Plan: Prepare a comprehensive business plan that outlines your vision, market analysis, financial projections, and repayment strategies.

Collateral: Depending on the loan type, lenders may require collateral such as real estate, inventory, or equipment.

Grants and Government Programs:

Government organizations and private foundations often offer grants and funding programs to support specific industries, innovations, or social initiatives. Here are a few steps to consider when seeking grants:

Research: Identify grant programs that align with your business sector or objectives.

Eligibility Criteria: Ensure your business meets the specific requirements outlined by the granting organization.

Application Process: Prepare a compelling grant proposal, including a detailed budget and a persuasive case for your project's impact.

Angel Investors:

Angel investors are individuals or groups who provide capital in exchange for equity ownership in your business. Consider these tips when approaching angel investors:

Networking: Attend entrepreneurial events and join startup communities to meet potential angel investors.

Pitch Deck: Create a concise and compelling pitch deck that outlines your business concept, market potential, and financial projections.

Due Diligence: Expect angel investors to conduct thorough research and due diligence before making an investment decision.

Venture Capital:

Venture capital firms invest in high-growth potential businesses in exchange for equity. Here's what to keep in mind when pursuing venture capital:

Scalability: Venture capitalists seek businesses with the potential for rapid growth and substantial returns.

Pitch Preparation: Craft a polished pitch deck and be prepared for rigorous questioning and negotiations.

Equity Dilution: Understand that securing venture capital involves giving up a portion of your ownership and control.

Funding your business venture is a critical aspect of its success. Explore the various options discussed in this chapter and assess which ones align best with your business goals and financial situation. Remember, combining multiple funding sources or utilizing alternative methods like crowdfunding can also be effective. Careful planning, preparation, and persistence will increase your chances of securing the funding necessary to bring your business venture to life. Additionally, it's important to maintain open lines of communication with your investors or lenders and fulfill your financial obligations according to the agreed-upon terms.

Crowdfunding:

Crowdfunding platforms have gained popularity as a way to raise capital from a large pool of individuals who believe in your business idea. Here's how to leverage crowdfunding effectively:

Platform Selection: Research and choose a crowdfunding platform that aligns with your business niche and fundraising goals.

Compelling Campaign: Create a captivating campaign that clearly communicates your vision, unique selling proposition, and potential impact.

Rewards or Equity: Determine whether you will offer rewards to backers or consider equity crowdfunding, which involves selling shares of your business.

Incubators and Accelerators:

Incubators and accelerators are organizations that provide mentorship, resources, and sometimes funding to early-stage businesses. Consider the following when exploring incubator or accelerator programs:

Research: Look for programs that specialize in your industry or offer the resources you need to grow your business.

Application Process: Prepare a strong application, highlighting your business concept, team, and growth potential.

Networking and Mentorship: Take advantage of the networking opportunities and guidance provided by experienced entrepreneurs and industry experts.

Strategic Partnerships and Joint Ventures:

Collaborating with established businesses through strategic partnerships or joint ventures can provide both financial support and valuable expertise. Consider these steps when pursuing strategic partnerships:

Identify Potential Partners: Look for businesses that complement your offerings or have a similar target audience.

Value Proposition: Clearly articulate the benefits of the partnership and how it will drive mutual growth and success.

Legal Agreements: Work with legal professionals to draft comprehensive agreements that outline the terms, responsibilities, and financial arrangements.

Alternative Funding Sources:

In addition to the traditional options mentioned earlier, consider exploring alternative funding sources such as:

Peer-to-Peer Lending: Platforms that connect borrowers directly with individual lenders.

Revenue-Based Financing: Agreeing to repay a percentage of future revenue in exchange for immediate funding.

Business Competitions and Pitch Events: Participating in entrepreneurial competitions where you can win cash prizes or investment opportunities.

Funding your business venture is a multifaceted process that requires research, preparation, and persistence. By exploring and leveraging the various funding options available, you can secure the necessary capital to turn your entrepreneurial dreams into reality. Remember to carefully evaluate each option, consider the associated terms and requirements, and seek professional advice when needed. With the right funding in place, you can focus on growing your business and achieving long-term success.

Microloans and Community Development Financial Institutions (CDFIs):

Microloans are small loans offered by microfinance institutions or CDFIs to entrepreneurs and small businesses. These loans are typically easier to obtain than traditional bank loans and can be used for various business needs. Consider the following when exploring microloans:

Research CDFIs: Look for local or regional CDFIs that specialize in providing microloans to businesses in your community.

Application Process: Prepare a solid business plan and demonstrate your ability to repay the loan.

Technical Assistance: Some CDFIs provide additional support in the form of business education, mentorship, and networking opportunities.

Pre-Sales and Crowdfunding Pre-orders:

If you have a product-based business, you can generate funds by offering pre-sales or running a crowdfunding campaign that allows people to pre-order your product. This approach not only provides upfront capital but also validates market demand. Consider the following:

Compelling Marketing: Create an effective marketing campaign to generate buzz and attract potential customers.

Clear Incentives: Offer attractive incentives to encourage early adopters and backers to make pre-orders or pledges.

Fulfillment Planning: Ensure you have a solid plan in place to fulfill orders and meet customer expectations.

Small Business Administration (SBA) Loans:

The U.S. Small Business Administration offers several loan programs designed to support small businesses. These loans are provided by participating lenders and partially guaranteed by the SBA. Here are a few key points to consider:

Program Research: Explore SBA loan programs such as the 7(a) Loan Program or the Microloan Program to find the best fit for your business.

Eligibility Criteria: Understand the requirements and qualifications for each program, such as credit history, collateral, and business size.

Application Assistance: The SBA provides resources and assistance through its network of Small Business Development Centers (SBDCs) to help with the loan application process.

Corporate Sponsorship:

If your business aligns with the objectives or values of a larger corporation, you can seek sponsorship or partnership opportunities. Corporate sponsors can provide financial support, marketing exposure, and access to their customer base. Consider the following when approaching potential corporate sponsors:

Research: Identify companies that have a vested interest in your industry or target market.

Value Proposition: Clearly articulate the benefits and value your business can offer to the potential sponsor.

Networking: Attend industry conferences, trade shows, and networking events where you can connect with decision-makers from target companies.

Personal and Professional Networks:

Leveraging your personal and professional networks can often lead to unexpected funding opportunities. Be proactive in reaching out to individuals who may be interested in investing or partnering with you. Consider these tips:

Networking: Attend industry events, join professional organizations, and build relationships with potential investors or mentors.

Pitching: Prepare a concise and persuasive pitch to present your business idea to your network, emphasizing the potential return on investment.

Referrals: Leverage your existing connections to seek introductions to potential investors or partners who may have an interest in your business.

Funding your business venture requires exploring a wide range of options and being resourceful in finding the right financial support. By considering these additional funding avenues and thinking creatively, you can increase your chances of securing the necessary capital to fuel your business growth. Remember, perseverance and adaptability are key as you navigate the funding landscape and work towards achieving your entrepreneurial goals.

Some suppliers or vendors may be willing to extend credit terms to help finance your business. This arrangement allows you to acquire necessary inventory or materials without immediate payment, giving you time to generate revenue before settling the balance. Consider the following:

Relationship Building: Nurture strong relationships with your suppliers or vendors, demonstrating your trustworthiness and commitment to their products or services.

Negotiation: Discuss the possibility of extended payment terms or trade credit arrangements that align with your business needs.

Timely Payments: Honor your payment commitments promptly to maintain a positive relationship and potentially negotiate more favorable terms in the future.

Business incubators provide a supportive environment for early-stage startups, offering resources, mentorship, and sometimes even financial support. Participating in an incubation program can help you access funding opportunities and guidance specific to your industry. Consider the following:

Explore business incubators that focus on your industry or target market.

Submit a comprehensive application, highlighting your business concept, market potential, and growth plans.

Assess the resources and funding opportunities offered by the incubator, as well as the level of support and mentorship available.

If your business requires expensive equipment or machinery, leasing or equipment financing can be a viable option. This allows you to obtain the necessary assets without the upfront cost of purchasing. Consider the following:

Research multiple leasing companies or equipment financing options to find the best rates and terms.

Evaluate whether leasing or financing the equipment aligns better with your long-term business goals.

Understand the responsibilities and costs associated with equipment maintenance and potential upgrades.

Collaborating with other businesses through strategic alliances or joint ventures can provide shared resources and funding opportunities. By pooling together expertise and resources, you can access capital and accelerate growth. Consider the following:

Identify businesses that can bring complementary skills, resources, or customer bases to the partnership.

Ensure alignment in terms of long-term objectives, growth strategies, and financial expectations.

Work with legal professionals to draft comprehensive agreements that outline the terms, responsibilities, and financial arrangements.

Look for grants specific to your industry or business sector, as well as business competitions that offer cash prizes or investment opportunities. These funding sources can provide a boost to your venture while gaining exposure and validation. Consider the following:

Explore grant opportunities from government agencies, nonprofit organizations, and corporate foundations that align with your business.

Polish your business plan, pitch deck, and presentation skills to stand out in competitions.

Take advantage of networking opportunities during competitions to connect with potential investors, mentors, or partners.

With an abundance of funding options available, it's crucial to carefully assess and prioritize which avenues align best with your business needs and goals. By tapping into various funding sources, leveraging networks, and presenting a compelling business case, you can increase your chances of securing the necessary funding to fuel your business venture. Remember to approach each opportunity with thorough research, preparedness, and professionalism, and be open to creative solutions that can help bring your entrepreneurial dreams to fruition.

In life, we often hear the adage, "You are the average of the five people you spend the most time with." This statement holds a profound truth—our environment and the people we surround ourselves with have a tremendous impact on our lives. The relationships we cultivate shape our thoughts, attitudes, behaviors, and ultimately, our success or failure. In this chapter, we delve into the importance of surrounding yourself with the right people and the transformative effect they can have on your journey.

The Law of Association states that we become like the people we surround ourselves with. Our thoughts, beliefs, and behaviors are strongly influenced by those around us. By associating with positive, motivated, and ambitious individuals, we are more likely to adopt their mindset and drive towards success.

Our emotions are contagious, and the people we interact with can either uplift or drain us. When we surround ourselves with supportive, encouraging, and uplifting individuals, we create an environment that fosters emotional well-being. They inspire us, offer guidance during difficult times, and provide a strong support system that contributes to our overall happiness.

The right people in our lives challenge us to become better versions of ourselves. They push us outside our comfort zones, encourage us to pursue our dreams, and provide valuable feedback that helps us grow. By surrounding ourselves with individuals who have achieved what we aspire to, we gain access to their knowledge, experiences, and expertise, accelerating our personal growth and development.

Having a circle of motivated and ambitious individuals can significantly impact our level of motivation. When we witness others striving for success and achieving their goals, we are inspired to do the same. Moreover, our circle can hold us accountable for our actions, helping us stay focused and committed to our endeavors.

The right people in our lives introduce us to new networks and opportunities. Through their connections, we gain access to a broader range of resources, mentors, and potential collaborators. Networking with like-minded individuals opens doors that may have otherwise remained closed, increasing our chances of success in various domains.

Take a critical look at your current relationships and evaluate their impact on your life. Identify individuals who uplift and inspire you, and those who drain your energy or hold you back from reaching your potential.

Define the qualities and values you seek in the people you want to surround yourself with. Look for individuals who are positive, supportive, ambitious, and align with your goals and aspirations.

Actively seek out opportunities to connect with individuals who possess the traits you desire. Join communities, attend events, or engage in activities aligned with your interests. Foster these relationships by offering support, being a good listener, and demonstrating your commitment to their success as well.

Surrounding yourself with the right people is a transformative decision that can shape the trajectory of your life. The influence of your inner circle goes beyond mere companionship; it affects your mindset, personal growth, motivation, and opportunities. Choose your inner circle wisely, and strive to create an environment that propels you towards success, happiness, and fulfillment. Remember, the people you surround yourself with can either lift you up to great heights or hold you back, so choose wisely and embrace the power of your inner circle.

Sometimes, we find ourselves surrounded by people who bring us down or hinder our progress. It can be challenging, but it is crucial to recognize when certain relationships are toxic or detrimental to our well-being. Letting go of negative influences is a necessary step in creating space for positive and supportive individuals.

While it is important to surround ourselves with like-minded individuals, it is equally crucial to embrace diversity in perspectives. Engaging with people who have different backgrounds, experiences, and viewpoints can broaden our horizons, challenge our assumptions, and foster creativity. Embracing diversity within our inner circle enables us to grow and learn from one another.

Maintaining healthy boundaries is essential when building the right inner circle. It is important to clearly communicate our values, goals, and expectations to those around us. By setting boundaries, we protect our well-being, maintain focus on our aspirations, and create an environment that supports our growth.

Being part of someone else's inner circle comes with the responsibility to support and uplift them. Just as we benefit from positive relationships, we have the opportunity to be a positive influence in someone else's life. By offering encouragement, providing guidance, and celebrating their successes, we contribute to their growth and well-being.

Accountability is a powerful tool for personal development. In a trusted inner circle, we can hold each other accountable for our actions, goals, and commitments. By providing constructive feedback and holding others to high standards, we create an environment of growth and accountability.

Building meaningful relationships requires a willingness to give and receive. It is important to be open to receiving support, advice, and guidance from others within our inner circle. By being receptive to their contributions, we foster mutual trust, respect, and collaboration.

Surrounding yourself with the right people is a conscious choice that requires self-awareness, reflection, and effort. It is a dynamic process that involves evaluating current relationships, identifying the desired traits, and actively seeking connections with individuals who uplift, inspire, and challenge you. Remember, the power of your inner circle extends beyond personal growth—it can shape your mindset, motivation, and opportunities. Embrace the journey of building the right inner circle, and in turn, strive to be a positive influence in someone else's life. Together, we can create supportive networks that propel us towards success, fulfillment, and lasting happiness.

In today's dynamic and competitive business landscape, success often hinges on the collective efforts of a high-performing team. Building a winning team is not just about gathering talented individuals; it is about fostering synergy, collaboration, and a shared vision. In this chapter, we will explore the key principles and strategies for assembling a winning team that can drive your business towards exceptional results.

Begin by defining a clear and compelling purpose for your team. Outline the team's mission, values, and objectives, ensuring that everyone understands and aligns with the overarching goals of the business. A shared purpose serves as the foundation for a motivated and focused team.

Establish specific, measurable, attainable, relevant, and time-bound (SMART) goals for your team. Clearly communicate these goals, ensuring that they are challenging yet realistic. SMART goals provide a roadmap for the team, fostering clarity and a sense of direction.

Determine the key competencies and skills required for your team's success. Look beyond technical expertise and consider qualities such as adaptability, teamwork, problem-solving, and communication skills. Seek individuals who not only possess the necessary qualifications but also fit well within the team's culture.

During the hiring process, conduct thorough interviews and assessments to evaluate candidates' qualifications, experiences, and cultural fit. Use behavioral and situational questions to gauge their problem-solving abilities, collaboration skills, and alignment with the team's values. Consider involving existing team members in the interview process to ensure compatibility and cultural fit.

Create an environment of psychological safety where team members feel comfortable expressing their ideas, taking risks, and challenging the status quo. Encourage open and honest communication, and emphasize that mistakes are opportunities for learning and growth. When team members feel safe to share their thoughts, creativity and innovation thrive.

Effective communication is vital for team success. Encourage regular and transparent communication among team members through various channels such as meetings, emails, and collaborative tools. Foster active listening and provide constructive feedback to enhance understanding and resolve conflicts promptly.

Trust is the cornerstone of any winning team. Lead by example, demonstrate integrity, and encourage transparency within the team. Foster an environment where trust is nurtured through open communication, mutual respect, and honoring commitments. Trust enables team members to rely on one another and work collaboratively towards shared goals.

Create opportunities for collaboration through team-building activities, cross-functional projects, and shared responsibilities. Encourage diverse perspectives and create a culture that values and respects the contributions of each team member. Foster a sense of belonging and create platforms for sharing ideas, brainstorming, and problem-solving collectively.

Regularly recognize and celebrate the achievements and contributions of individual team members and the team as a whole. Publicly acknowledge their efforts, provide constructive feedback, and reward exceptional performance. This fosters a positive work environment and motivates team members to excel.

Support the growth and development of your team members by providing opportunities for training, mentorship, and advancement. Encourage them to enhance their skills, pursue professional certifications, and stay updated with industry trends. Investing in their professional development demonstrates your commitment to their success and strengthens their capabilities, benefiting both the individual team members and the overall team's performance.

Promote a supportive and inclusive team culture where everyone feels valued and respected. Encourage collaboration, teamwork, and a willingness to help one another. Foster a positive work environment by addressing conflicts promptly, promoting work-life balance, and prioritizing employee well-being.

Recognize and embrace the value of diversity within your team. Foster an inclusive environment where different perspectives and backgrounds are celebrated. Encourage open discussions and consider diverse viewpoints to drive innovation and creative problem-solving.

Regularly evaluate the team's performance, progress towards goals, and individual contributions. Use performance metrics and feedback mechanisms to identify areas of improvement and provide guidance for individual and team development.

In a rapidly changing business landscape, it is crucial to remain agile and adapt quickly. Encourage a culture of continuous learning and improvement, where team members are encouraged to embrace change, experiment, and find innovative solutions to challenges.

Building a winning team requires intentional effort, strategic planning, and ongoing commitment. By defining your team's purpose, hiring the right talent, fostering collaboration and communication, cultivating trust, recognizing and developing talent, nurturing a positive team culture, and continuously evaluating and improving, you can create a cohesive and high-performing team that propels your business towards success. Remember, a winning team is not just a collection of individual talents; it is a unified force that leverages each member's strengths, supports one another, and shares a common vision of excellence.

As the leader of the team, it is essential to provide inspirational and visionary leadership. Lead by example, demonstrating passion, commitment, and a strong work ethic. Inspire your team members by communicating a compelling vision, setting high standards, and fostering a culture of excellence.

Empower your team members by delegating responsibilities and trusting them to make decisions. Encourage autonomy and ownership over their work, allowing them to showcase their skills and contribute meaningfully. Provide support and guidance when needed, but also create opportunities for them to grow and excel independently.

Conflicts are inevitable in any team, but it is essential to address them promptly and constructively. Encourage open dialogue, active listening, and empathy when resolving conflicts. Foster a problem-solving mindset that focuses on finding win-win solutions and maintaining healthy working relationships.

In a fast-paced business environment, resilience is key to overcoming challenges and maintaining team morale. Foster a resilient mindset within your team by encouraging a positive outlook, providing support during difficult times, and promoting a culture of learning from setbacks. Help team members develop their emotional intelligence and coping mechanisms to navigate obstacles and bounce back stronger.

Engage in regular team-building activities to foster stronger bonds and enhance collaboration. These activities can include team outings, workshops, and exercises that promote trust, communication, and camaraderie among team members.

Take the time to celebrate milestones and successes as a team. Recognize and reward achievements, both big and small, to boost team morale and motivation. Celebrating together not only acknowledges the hard work of individuals but also strengthens the team's sense of unity and accomplishment.

Building a winning team in business is a dynamic process that requires consistent effort and a focus on developing a collaborative, empowered, and resilient group. By providing purpose, hiring the right talent, fostering effective communication, building trust, recognizing and developing individuals, nurturing a positive team culture, and continuously evaluating and improving, you can create a team that excels and achieves outstanding results. Remember, a winning team is more than the sum of its parts—it is a cohesive unit that thrives on shared values, trust, and a collective commitment to excellence.

Creating a Memorable Identity

"First impressions are lasting impressions," a phrase we often hear and instinctively understand the weight it carries. Whether it's meeting someone for the first time, attending a job interview, or entering a new environment, the importance of first impressions cannot be overstated. In this chapter, we delve into the significance of first impressions, exploring their impact on personal relationships, professional opportunities, and overall perceptions.

Humans are inherently social beings, and from the moment we interact with others, our minds start forming impressions. These initial encounters set the tone for future interactions and influence how we perceive and respond to individuals or situations. Within a matter of seconds, our brains unconsciously assess body language, facial expressions, and vocal tone, creating a snapshot impression that can be difficult to reverse.

In the realm of personal relationships, first impressions play a pivotal role. Whether it's making new friends, romantic connections, or even meeting potential in-laws, the initial judgment formed can have a lasting impact. Positive first impressions often create a foundation of trust, warmth, and comfort, enabling stronger connections to develop. On the other hand, negative first impressions can be challenging to overcome, leading to strained relationships or missed opportunities for deeper connections.

In the realm of professional life, first impressions carry immense weight. Job interviews, networking events, and meetings with colleagues or clients all rely heavily on the impressions we make. Research suggests that employers often form opinions about job candidates within the first few minutes of an interview, emphasizing the importance of a strong initial impression. Dressing appropriately, displaying confidence, and demonstrating effective communication skills are all factors that contribute to making a positive impact and potentially securing career opportunities.

Psychologists have identified the primacy effect, which suggests that individuals tend to remember information encountered early on better than what they encounter later. This concept applies to first impressions as well. The initial impression we make tends to stick in the minds of others, shaping their perception of us moving forward. This phenomenon further highlights the significance of starting off on the right foot, as subsequent interactions may be influenced by the initial impression.

While it is possible to overcome negative first impressions, it often requires considerable effort and time. People may be hesitant to give second chances or may be influenced by the initial judgment they formed. It is crucial to recognize the impact of first impressions and proactively work towards dispelling any negative perceptions by demonstrating consistent positive qualities and building trust over time.

Creating a positive first impression should not be mistaken for putting on a facade or pretending to be someone you're not. Authenticity is a vital component of building genuine connections. It is important to align our behavior, values, and intentions with our true selves. When our external presentation and internal disposition are congruent, we create a strong foundation for building meaningful relationships.

First impressions serve as the entry point to personal and professional connections, leaving a lasting impact on our lives. They shape perceptions, influence opportunities, and affect the way others perceive us. Being aware of the significance of first impressions allows us to be more mindful of our actions, presentation, and communication, ensuring that we make a positive impact right from the start. By cultivating authenticity, displaying confidence, and making a genuine effort to connect with others, we can maximize the benefits of first impressions and foster deeper, more fulfilling relationships in all areas of our lives.

The study of first impressions has long fascinated psychologists, as it provides valuable insights into human cognition, social interactions, and the complex nature of perception. In this chapter, we delve into the psychology behind first impressions, exploring the underlying processes, cognitive biases, and psychological mechanisms that shape our initial judgments of others.

One of the key psychological phenomena associated with first impressions is the primacy effect, as mentioned in the previous chapter. This cognitive bias suggests that people tend to rely heavily on the first information they receive when forming an impression. Initial encounters serve as a mental anchor, influencing subsequent judgments and perceptions. Additionally, the halo effect, a cognitive bias where a positive trait or characteristic influences the perception of other qualities, further reinforces the importance of first impressions.

Non-verbal cues play a significant role in shaping first impressions. Research has shown that body language, facial expressions, and tone of voice contribute more to the impression we form of someone than the actual words spoken. Gestures, posture, eye contact, and even microexpressions can convey a wealth of information about a person's emotional state, confidence level, and overall demeanor. Understanding and interpreting these non-verbal signals is essential for accurately assessing others during initial encounters.

In many cases, first impressions are formed rapidly, often within seconds or fractions of a second. This process is known as thin-slicing, where individuals make quick judgments based on limited information. Thin-slicing allows us to efficiently navigate social situations by relying on automatic, intuitive processes. However, these rapid judgments can also be prone to biases and inaccuracies, as they are influenced by stereotypes, cultural conditioning, and personal experiences.

Stereotypes, deeply ingrained societal beliefs or assumptions about certain groups, can significantly impact the formation of first impressions. When encountering someone from a particular social, cultural, or demographic group, our brains often rely on preexisting schemas, mental frameworks that organize and interpret information. These schemas can lead to biased judgments and reinforce stereotypes, making it challenging to form objective and accurate first impressions.

Confirmation bias, a cognitive bias that influences how we interpret information to support our existing beliefs, can further affect the psychology of first impressions. Once we form an initial impression, we tend to seek out and prioritize information that confirms our preconceived notions, while disregarding or downplaying contradictory evidence. This bias can solidify our first impressions and make it challenging to revise our opinions, even when presented with new information.

Implicit personality theories are another psychological concept that influences how we form first impressions. These theories consist of our beliefs about how certain traits or characteristics tend to coexist in individuals. For example, we might assume that someone who is physically attractive is also friendly or intelligent. Implicit personality theories guide our perception and judgment of others, shaping our initial impressions based on inferred qualities and associations.

Context plays a significant role in the psychology of first impressions. The environment, social setting, and situational factors can influence the weight we assign to different cues and traits when forming an impression. For instance, someone might be perceived as confident and assertive in a business setting but appear arrogant or aggressive in a social gathering. Recognizing the contextual factors at play allows for a more nuanced understanding of first impressions and reduces the risk of making overly generalized judgments.

The psychology of first impressions is a complex interplay of cognitive processes, biases, and social factors. Understanding these underlying mechanisms enables us to navigate and interpret initial encounters more effectively.

In the highly competitive world of business, establishing a memorable brand is not just a luxury but a necessity. A brand is more than just a logo or a slogan; it encompasses the entire identity of a business and how it is perceived by customers, partners, and stakeholders. In this chapter, we explore the reasons why it is crucial for businesses to invest in creating a memorable brand that leaves a lasting impact.

In today's crowded marketplace, where consumers are inundated with choices, a memorable brand is essential for differentiation.

A strong brand sets a business apart from its competitors by communicating its unique value proposition, core values, and distinct personality. It allows customers to make an emotional connection and perceive the business as offering something special or different. This differentiation helps create a competitive advantage, attracting customers who resonate with the brand's message and increasing loyalty.

A memorable brand inspires trust and credibility among consumers. When customers recognize a brand and have positive associations with it, they are more likely to trust its products or services. A well-established brand with a track record of delivering quality and consistency instills confidence in customers, making them more willing to engage with the business. Trust is a fundamental building block of customer relationships, and a memorable brand can help establish that trust from the outset.

Creating a memorable brand is a powerful way to foster customer loyalty and advocacy. A brand that consistently delivers on its promises and meets customer expectations builds a loyal customer base. These loyal customers not only become repeat buyers but also serve as brand ambassadors, spreading positive word-of-mouth recommendations to their networks. When customers identify with a brand's values and have a positive emotional connection, they are more likely to become advocates, driving new customers to the business.

Memorable brands have the ability to forge emotional connections with consumers. Emotions play a significant role in decision-making, and brands that evoke positive emotions are more likely to be remembered and recalled when a need arises. By creating a unique brand identity that resonates with customers on an emotional level, businesses can leave a lasting impression and increase brand recall. This emotional connection leads to a deeper relationship with customers, fostering loyalty and repeat business.

Establishing a memorable brand can enable a business to command premium pricing for its products or services. When customers perceive a brand as superior or offering unique value, they are often willing to pay a premium for that perceived quality. A strong brand with a reputation for excellence and innovation can justify higher prices, leading to increased profitability and financial success.

A memorable brand not only appeals to customers but also attracts and retains top talent. In today's competitive job market, employees are increasingly looking for more than just a paycheck. They seek companies with a compelling brand story, a strong purpose, and a positive reputation. A memorable brand can help attract top talent who align with the brand's values and mission. Moreover, a strong brand identity and culture can contribute to higher employee engagement, satisfaction, and retention.

In a business landscape where competition is fierce, establishing a memorable brand is crucial for success. A memorable brand differentiates a business, builds trust and credibility, fosters customer loyalty and advocacy, creates emotional connections, enables premium pricing, and attracts top talent. Investing in brand building is a long-term strategy that pays dividends by setting a business apart from the competition, forging strong customer relationships, and driving sustainable growth.

Now that we understand the importance of establishing a memorable brand in business, it's essential to explore the strategies and actions that can help businesses create a lasting brand identity. In this chapter, we delve into practical approaches for building a memorable brand that resonates with customers and leaves a lasting impact.

Start by defining your brand identity, which encompasses your brand's values, mission, personality, and target audience. Understand what sets your business apart and identify the unique value proposition you offer. This clarity will guide all aspects of your brand building efforts, ensuring consistency and coherence across various touchpoints.

Humans are wired to connect through stories. Develop a compelling brand narrative that communicates your brand's history, purpose, and the problems you aim to solve. Your brand story should evoke emotions, capture the imagination, and engage your target audience. Use storytelling techniques to create a memorable and relatable brand experience.

Create a visually appealing and consistent brand identity that includes a logo, color palette, typography, and visual elements. These visual components should be aligned with your brand's personality, values, and target audience. Consistency across all brand collateral, including website, packaging, marketing materials, and social media, helps reinforce brand recognition and recall.

Focus on delivering exceptional brand experiences at every touchpoint. Ensure that each interaction a customer has with your brand is aligned with your brand promise. From customer service to product packaging, strive for consistency and excellence. A positive brand experience fosters customer loyalty, word-of-mouth referrals, and long-term brand advocacy.

In today's digital age, an authentic online presence is vital for brand building. Develop a robust online strategy that includes a well-designed website, active social media profiles, and consistent messaging across digital channels. Engage with your audience, respond to their feedback, and provide valuable content that aligns with your brand values.

Create opportunities for meaningful engagement with your audience. Encourage customer feedback, respond to inquiries promptly, and actively participate in relevant conversations within your industry. Build a community around your brand by fostering two-way communication and creating a sense of belonging.

Collaborate with complementary brands or influencers to expand your reach and tap into new audiences. Strategic partnerships can help amplify your brand's message and create mutually beneficial relationships. Choose partners that align with your brand values and have a similar target audience to maximize the impact of these collaborations.

Stay ahead of the curve by continuously evolving and innovating. Monitor industry trends, listen to customer feedback, and be open to adapting your brand strategy as needed. Embrace innovation to offer new and exciting products, services, or experiences that align with your brand identity. By staying relevant and fresh, your brand will remain memorable and resonate with evolving consumer preferences.

Building a memorable brand requires careful planning, consistent execution, and an unwavering commitment to delivering value and exceptional experiences. By defining your brand identity, crafting a compelling brand story, maintaining a consistent visual identity, emphasizing brand experience, establishing an authentic online presence, engaging with your audience, collaborating strategically, and continuously evolving, you can create a brand that stands out, resonates with customers, and leaves a lasting impression in the minds and hearts of your target audience.

Once you have established a memorable brand, the work doesn't end there. To ensure its longevity and continued impact, it is essential to focus on maintaining and reinforcing your brand. In this chapter, we explore strategies and tactics for effectively managing and strengthening your brand over time.

Consistency is a fundamental element of brand maintenance. Ensure that your brand is consistently represented across all touchpoints, including visual elements, messaging, tone of voice, and customer experiences. Consistency builds trust, reinforces brand recognition, and fosters a sense of reliability and authenticity.

Regularly monitor and assess how your brand is perceived in the marketplace. Keep an eye on customer feedback, conduct surveys or focus groups, and pay attention to social media conversations. Actively listen to your audience to gain insights into their perceptions, needs, and expectations. This feedback loop allows you to address any issues, make necessary adjustments, and continuously align your brand with customer expectations.

While consistency is crucial, it is equally important to evolve your brand with purpose. Stay attuned to changes in the market, consumer preferences, and industry trends. Strive to be innovative and adaptable while maintaining the core essence of your brand. Thoughtfully introduce updates or enhancements to keep your brand fresh, relevant, and in tune with the evolving needs of your target audience.

Consistently deliver on the promises made by your brand. This includes the quality of your products or services, customer service interactions, and overall brand experience. Meeting or exceeding customer expectations builds trust and reinforces the positive perception of your brand. Make it a priority to align internal operations and processes with your brand values to ensure a consistent and exceptional customer experience.

Your employees play a vital role in reinforcing your brand. They are the face of your brand and have the power to influence customer perceptions. Foster a strong internal brand culture by ensuring that your employees understand and embody your brand values and messaging. Empower them to be brand ambassadors, providing them with the tools, training, and support they need to consistently represent the brand in their interactions with customers and stakeholders.

Identify and nurture brand advocates—customers who are passionate about your brand and actively promote it to others. Engage with these advocates, acknowledge their support, and provide incentives for their loyalty and advocacy. Encourage user-generated content, testimonials, and positive reviews to amplify the reach and impact of your brand. Leverage the power of word-of-mouth marketing through your brand advocates.

As communication channels evolve, ensure that your brand is present and relevant across various platforms. Stay abreast of emerging technologies and social media trends to effectively engage with your target audience. Adapt your messaging and content strategies to suit different platforms while maintaining consistent brand elements and values. Be agile and open to exploring new communication channels that align with your brand strategy.

Maintaining and reinforcing a memorable brand requires ongoing effort, vigilance, and adaptation. By prioritizing consistency, actively monitoring brand perception, evolving with purpose, delivering on brand promises, cultivating employee brand ambassadors, engaging and rewarding brand advocates, and adapting to changing communication channels, you can effectively manage and strengthen your brand's impact over time. A well-maintained and reinforced brand not only builds customer loyalty but also positions your business for long-term success in a competitive marketplace.

Protecting and preserving your memorable brand is essential to safeguarding its value, reputation, and distinctiveness. In this chapter, we explore strategies and considerations for brand protection, including legal aspects, brand monitoring, and proactive measures to maintain the integrity of your brand.

One of the foundational steps in protecting your brand is to register trademarks for your brand name, logo, and other distinctive elements. Consult with legal professionals specializing in intellectual property to ensure proper trademark registration in relevant jurisdictions. Trademark protection provides legal recourse against unauthorized use or infringement, reinforcing the exclusivity and recognition of your brand.

Establish a brand monitoring system to actively monitor online and offline channels for any unauthorized use, counterfeiting, or infringement of your brand. Utilize automated tools, employ manual searches, and monitor social media platforms, websites, marketplaces, and industry publications. Promptly address any instances of brand misuse to mitigate potential damage and protect your brand's reputation.

When instances of unauthorized use or infringement are identified, take prompt action to enforce your intellectual property rights. This may involve sending cease and desist letters, pursuing legal action, or working with intellectual property professionals to resolve the issue. Proactive enforcement sends a clear message that you are committed to protecting your brand and its integrity.

Develop comprehensive brand guidelines that outline the proper use of your brand's visual elements, messaging, and tone of voice. These guidelines ensure consistent and accurate representation of your brand across all communication channels, both internally and externally. Provide employees, partners, and stakeholders with access to these guidelines to maintain brand consistency and prevent misrepresentation.

When collaborating with partners, licensees, or distributors, establish clear agreements that define the terms of brand usage and protect your intellectual property rights. Conduct due diligence to ensure that partners align with your brand values and have a reputation for maintaining brand integrity. Regularly communicate and monitor compliance with brand guidelines to ensure consistent representation.

Develop a robust crisis management plan to address potential threats to your brand's reputation. Prepare strategies and protocols for responding to crises, managing negative publicity, and mitigating reputational damage. Swift and transparent communication during challenging times can help preserve brand trust and loyalty.

Maintain a proactive approach to brand building and innovation to stay ahead of competitors and maintain the relevance of your brand. Regularly assess market trends, customer preferences, and industry developments to identify opportunities for brand expansion or refinement. Continuously evolve and adapt your brand strategy while staying true to the core values and essence of your brand.

Protecting and preserving your memorable brand is an ongoing process that requires strategic planning, diligent monitoring, and proactive measures. By registering trademarks, implementing brand monitoring systems, enforcing intellectual property rights, establishing brand guidelines, collaborating with trusted partners, managing crises effectively, and fostering continuous brand building and innovation, you can safeguard the value and reputation of your brand. By prioritizing brand protection, you position your business for sustained success and maintain the trust and loyalty of your customers in the long run.

Converting Customers

In the competitive world of business, reaching and converting customers is crucial for the success and growth of any organization. It requires a strategic approach and an understanding of the target audience. In this chapter, we will explore effective techniques and strategies that can help you reach and convert customers for your business.

Before you can reach and convert customers, it's important to identify and define your target audience. Who are your ideal customers? What are their demographics, interests, and pain points? By understanding your target audience, you can tailor your marketing efforts to effectively reach and resonate with them.

A value proposition is a clear statement that explains how your product or service solves a customer's problem or fulfills a need better than the competition. It should communicate the unique benefits and advantages that your business offers. Craft a compelling value proposition that appeals to your target audience and differentiates your business from competitors.

In today's digital age, having a strong online presence is essential. Create a professional website that showcases your products or services and provides valuable information to potential customers. Optimize your website for search engines to improve its visibility. Additionally, establish a presence on relevant social media platforms and engage with your audience through regular content updates, interactions, and targeted advertising.

Content marketing is a powerful tool for reaching and engaging customers. Create high-quality, informative content that educates and entertains your target audience. Develop a content strategy that includes blog posts, articles, videos, infographics, and podcasts. Share this content on your website and social media platforms to attract and engage potential customers. Consider guest blogging and collaborations with influencers or industry experts to expand your reach.

Optimizing your online content for search engines can help you reach customers who are actively searching for solutions. Research relevant keywords and incorporate them into your website content, blog posts, and metadata. Focus on creating valuable, user-friendly content that addresses popular search queries. Additionally, ensure that your website is mobile-friendly and optimized for fast loading speeds.

Paid advertising can be an effective way to reach a larger audience and generate leads. Consider using platforms like Google Ads, social media advertising, and display advertising to target specific demographics and interests. Set clear goals, monitor your campaigns regularly, and make data-driven adjustments to maximize your ROI.

Email marketing allows you to nurture relationships with potential customers and convert them into paying customers. Build an email list by offering valuable content, discounts, or exclusive offers in exchange for email addresses. Segment your email list based on customer interests and behaviors, and personalize your email campaigns accordingly. Provide relevant and engaging content, send targeted promotions, and track the performance of your email campaigns.

To convert potential customers into paying customers, focus on lead generation and conversion strategies. Offer valuable incentives such as free trials, samples, or consultations to capture contact information and initiate the sales process. Use persuasive and personalized follow-up communication to nurture leads and guide them through the buyer's journey. Implement effective sales techniques and provide exceptional customer service to increase conversion rates.

A robust CRM system can help you manage and nurture customer relationships effectively. Use a CRM tool to organize customer data, track interactions, and automate follow-ups. Implement personalized communication and targeted marketing campaigns based on customer preferences and purchase history. By maintaining strong relationships with existing customers, you can encourage repeat business and benefit from positive word-of-mouth referrals.

Reaching and converting customers is a continuous process that requires ongoing analysis, adaptation, and improvement. By defining your target audience, developing a compelling value proposition, building an online presence, implementing content marketing, utilizing SEO, paid advertising, email marketing, and focusing on lead generation and conversion, you can effectively reach and convert customers for your business. However, the process doesn't end there. Generating and maintaining customer interest requires a continuous effort. Here are a few additional strategies to help you in the ongoing process of generating and converting customers:

Encourage your satisfied customers to refer your business to their friends, family, and colleagues. Implement a referral program that rewards customers for successful referrals. Offer incentives such as discounts, exclusive offers, or even cash rewards. Referral programs can be a cost-effective way to expand your customer base and build trust through personal recommendations.

Leverage social proof to build credibility and trust with potential customers. Display testimonials, reviews, case studies, and success stories from satisfied customers on your website and social media platforms. Positive feedback and endorsements from existing customers can greatly influence potential customers' decision-making process.

Implement remarketing strategies to target customers who have shown interest in your products or services but have not converted yet. Use tracking pixels and cookies to show relevant ads to these potential customers as they browse other websites or social media platforms. By staying top of mind, you increase the chances of conversion.

Tailor your marketing messages and offers to individual customers whenever possible. Use data-driven insights to segment your audience and deliver personalized content, product recommendations, and promotions. Personalization creates a sense of connection and relevance, increasing the likelihood of customer engagement and conversion.

Regularly test and optimize your marketing campaigns to improve their effectiveness. A/B test different elements such as headlines, calls to action, visuals, and offers to identify the most compelling combinations. Analyze the data and make data-driven decisions to refine your strategies and maximize your conversion rates.

Actively engage with your audience on social media platforms. Respond promptly to comments, messages, and inquiries. Encourage user-generated content by running contests, hosting giveaways, or creating interactive campaigns. Engaging with your audience helps build relationships, fosters brand loyalty, and increases the chances of customer conversion.

Consider forming strategic partnerships or collaborations with complementary businesses or influencers in your industry. By leveraging their existing customer base and reach, you can expand your brand's exposure and attract new customers. Collaborative efforts such as co-branded campaigns, joint events, or cross-promotions can be mutually beneficial and lead to customer acquisition.

Remember, reaching and converting customers is an ongoing process that requires a combination of strategies, consistent effort, and adaptation to changing market dynamics. Continuously monitor and analyze your marketing efforts, gather feedback from customers, and stay updated on industry trends to stay ahead of the competition and maintain a steady stream of customers for your business.

Actively seek feedback from your customers to understand their needs, preferences, and pain points. Conduct surveys, collect reviews, and engage in social listening to gather valuable insights. Use this feedback to improve your products, services, and overall customer experience. Positive reviews can serve as powerful social proof, while addressing negative feedback demonstrates your commitment to customer satisfaction.

Implement customer loyalty programs to reward and retain your existing customer base. Offer exclusive discounts, rewards, or VIP benefits to loyal customers. By providing incentives for repeat purchases, you not only increase customer retention but also encourage them to become brand advocates, referring new customers to your business.

Position yourself and your business as a thought leader in your industry. Share valuable insights, industry trends, and expertise through blog posts, articles, podcasts, or webinars. By establishing yourself as a trusted authority, you can attract customers who value your knowledge and seek your products or services.

While online marketing is crucial, don't overlook the power of offline marketing strategies. Depending on your target audience and industry, consider traditional marketing channels such as print advertisements, direct mail campaigns, event sponsorships, or attending trade shows and conferences. These offline tactics can help you reach a different segment of customers and create a well-rounded marketing approach.

Once you've converted a customer, focus on building long-term relationships. Stay in touch through personalized email newsletters, special offers, or loyalty programs. Provide exceptional customer service, address any concerns promptly, and go the extra mile to exceed their expectations. By nurturing customer relationships, you can encourage repeat business and foster customer loyalty.

Regularly monitor and analyze the performance of your marketing efforts using analytics tools. Track key metrics such as website traffic, conversion rates, customer acquisition cost, and customer lifetime value. This data will help you identify areas for improvement, optimize your marketing strategies, and make informed decisions to drive better results.

Reaching and converting customers in business requires a multi-faceted approach that combines online and offline strategies, personalization, continuous testing, and a focus on building strong relationships with customers. By implementing these strategies and continuously adapting to the evolving market landscape, you can effectively reach your target audience, convert leads into customers, and foster long-term customer loyalty, driving the success and growth of your business.

Stay updated on market trends, industry innovations, and customer preferences through continuous market research. Monitor competitor strategies, industry publications, and consumer behavior to identify emerging opportunities and stay ahead of the curve. This information will help you refine your marketing tactics, adapt your messaging, and stay relevant in a dynamic business landscape.

Leverage the power of influencers to reach and engage your target audience. Identify influencers in your industry who have a strong following and align with your brand values. Collaborate with them to create sponsored content, reviews, or endorsements that can effectively promote your products or services. Influencer marketing can significantly expand your brand reach and credibility among their loyal followers.

Empower your customers with knowledge by providing educational resources related to your products or industry. Create informative guides, tutorials, or webinars that help customers understand the value and benefits of your offerings. By educating your customers, you build trust, establish your expertise, and increase the likelihood of conversion.

Consumers today are increasingly conscious of a business's social and environmental impact. Incorporate social responsibility into your marketing efforts by supporting charitable causes or engaging in sustainable practices. Communicate your commitment to these causes to resonate with socially conscious customers who align with your values. Cause marketing can help differentiate your brand and attract customers who prioritize ethical considerations.

Encourage satisfied customers to refer their friends and family through a structured customer referral program. Incentivize referrals with rewards or discounts for both the referrer and the referred customer. Referrals from existing customers have a higher chance of conversion, as they come with built-in trust and credibility.

Implement retargeting strategies to reach customers who have shown interest in your products but did not complete a purchase. Use targeted ads or personalized emails to remind them about the products they viewed or items left in their shopping cart. This tactic can help re-engage customers and prompt them to complete the purchase.

Deliver a seamless and exceptional customer experience at every touchpoint. Optimize your website for easy navigation, quick loading times, and mobile responsiveness. Streamline your checkout process to reduce friction and simplify the purchasing journey. Provide personalized recommendations and tailored messaging based on customer preferences and browsing history. A positive customer experience can significantly impact conversion rates and customer satisfaction.

Collaborate with complementary businesses to expand your reach and tap into new customer segments. Identify businesses that share a similar target audience but offer non-competing products or services. Explore joint marketing initiatives, co-branded campaigns, or bundled offerings to provide added value to customers and access new markets.

Remember, reaching and converting customers is an ongoing process that requires constant adaptation and innovation. Keep experimenting with new strategies, analyzing results, and refining your approach based on customer feedback and market insights. By continuously optimizing your marketing efforts, you can effectively reach and convert customers, driving sustainable business growth.

Navigating the Requirements

Accountability is the cornerstone of personal growth and success. It is the foundation upon which we build our character and integrity. When we take accountability for our actions, we acknowledge our role in the outcomes of our lives and take ownership of our choices. In this chapter, we will explore the profound importance of embracing accountability and how it can empower you to unlock your true potential.

Accountability is the recognition that our actions have consequences and that we are responsible for those consequences. It is about looking inward and acknowledging our strengths, weaknesses, and the impact we have on others. When we embrace accountability, we shift from being passive observers to active participants in our own lives.

Self-reflection is a critical component of accountability. It allows us to examine our thoughts, beliefs, and behaviors honestly. By taking the time to reflect, we gain insight into our motivations and patterns. Self-reflection empowers us to make better choices, learn from our mistakes, and grow as individuals.

Mistakes are inevitable in life, and accountability is the key to turning them into valuable learning experiences. When we take ownership of our mistakes, we can identify the underlying causes, learn from them, and make necessary changes to avoid repeating them in the future. Accountability allows us to view mistakes as opportunities for growth rather than sources of shame or regret.

Accountability is closely linked to trust and integrity. When we hold ourselves accountable, we demonstrate to others that we are reliable, honest, and committed to our words and actions. By consistently honoring our commitments and taking responsibility for our mistakes, we build trust with those around us, fostering stronger relationships and a positive reputation.

Taking accountability is an essential catalyst for personal growth. It enables us to identify areas where we need to improve and take proactive steps to develop ourselves. When we acknowledge our shortcomings, we can seek out resources, guidance, and support to overcome them. Embracing accountability opens the door to continuous learning and self-improvement.

Accountability is not limited to our individual journeys. It extends to our relationships as well. By taking accountability for our actions and their impact on others, we cultivate healthier, more meaningful connections. It allows us to resolve conflicts more effectively, communicate openly, and create a supportive environment for personal and collective growth.

Embracing accountability requires courage and resilience. It is easy to succumb to the temptation of making excuses or blaming others for our circumstances. However, true accountability empowers us to face challenges head-on, take ownership of our choices, and find creative solutions. It shifts the focus from external factors to our internal locus of control.

Taking accountability is a powerful choice that has the potential to transform our lives. By recognizing our responsibilities, learning from our mistakes, and striving for personal growth, we unlock our true potential. Embrace accountability as a guiding principle, and you will pave the way for a more fulfilling and successful journey ahead. Remember, accountability is not a burden but a liberating force that sets you on a path of empowerment and self-discovery.

Developing an accountability mindset is crucial for making lasting changes in our lives. Here are some strategies to cultivate and strengthen your accountability:

Clearly define your goals and aspirations. When you have a clear vision of what you want to achieve, it becomes easier to hold yourself accountable for taking the necessary actions to reach those goals.

Surround yourself with individuals who value accountability and encourage your growth. Share your goals and progress with them, and ask for their support in holding you accountable. A supportive network can provide guidance, motivation, and constructive feedback.

Regularly monitor and assess your progress towards your goals. Keep a journal, use a tracking app, or create visual reminders of your milestones. Tracking your progress not only helps you stay accountable but also provides a sense of accomplishment and momentum.

Develop habits and routines that promote self-discipline. Set clear boundaries, manage your time effectively, and prioritize tasks that align with your goals. Self-discipline allows you to overcome distractions, stay focused, and follow through on your commitments.

Embrace the fact that accountability does not mean perfection. We are all fallible, and setbacks are part of the journey. Learn to accept and learn from your mistakes without letting them discourage you. Use setbacks as opportunities to recalibrate and keep moving forward.

Celebrate your accomplishments, no matter how small. Recognize and reward yourself for the progress you have made. Celebrating achievements reinforces positive behaviors and motivates you to continue taking accountability for your actions.

Remember to be kind to yourself throughout the process. Acknowledge that taking accountability requires courage and vulnerability. Treat yourself with compassion and understanding, allowing room for growth and self-forgiveness.

Taking accountability is not always easy, but it is undoubtedly worth the effort. By embracing accountability, you empower yourself to shape your own destiny, learn from your experiences, and grow into the best version of yourself. Cultivate an accountability mindset, surround yourself with support, and make a conscious effort to hold yourself responsible for your choices and actions. As you embark on this transformative journey, remember that accountability is not a destination but a lifelong practice that will lead you towards personal fulfillment and success.

Running a business is a complex and dynamic endeavor. It requires making countless decisions, navigating uncertainties, and adapting to changing circumstances. In this chapter, we will delve into the importance of taking ownership of your decisions and actions in your business. By embracing ownership, you will unleash your entrepreneurial potential and set a solid foundation for sustainable success.

As a business owner, the power to make decisions rests in your hands. Embracing this power means taking full ownership of the choices you make. Recognize that each decision, whether big or small, has the potential to impact your business's trajectory. When you accept this responsibility, you become proactive in shaping your business's direction rather than being a passive observer.

Every decision you make has consequences. By taking ownership of your decisions, you acknowledge that you are accountable for the outcomes that follow. Understand that the success or failure of your business is directly tied to the quality of decisions you make. Embrace the opportunity to learn from both positive and negative outcomes, allowing them to inform your future choices.

Entrepreneurship inherently involves taking risks. When you take ownership of your decisions, you embrace the associated risks and responsibilities. Understand that the road to success is often paved with challenges and setbacks. Embrace the entrepreneurial spirit by embracing calculated risks and taking responsibility for the outcomes, regardless of the result.

Taking ownership of your decisions requires a commitment to continuous learning and growth. Recognize that you cannot possess all the knowledge and expertise needed to make every decision perfectly. Be open to seeking advice, guidance, and expertise from mentors, industry experts, and trusted advisors. Embrace a mindset of curiosity and humility to expand your knowledge base and make well-informed decisions.

Owning your decisions means accepting failures as learning opportunities. Instead of dwelling on mistakes or succumbing to self-doubt, adopt a growth mindset. Analyze failures objectively, identify the root causes, and take corrective action. Embrace the concept of iteration, where each setback becomes a stepping stone toward improvement. Learn from failures, adapt, and evolve your business strategies accordingly.

Ownership requires taking initiative and being proactive in driving your business forward. Don't wait for external circumstances or market forces to dictate your path. Take charge, set ambitious goals, and create a clear action plan. Hold yourself accountable for executing that plan, tracking progress, and making necessary adjustments along the way. Ownership fuels a sense of empowerment and fuels your business's momentum.

As a business owner, you play a pivotal role in shaping the company culture. By taking ownership of your decisions, you set an example for your employees and foster a culture of accountability. Communicate the importance of ownership, encourage autonomy, and empower your team to make decisions within their areas of responsibility. A strong culture of ownership enhances employee engagement, fosters innovation, and drives overall business success.

In the dynamic business landscape, the ability to adapt and pivot is crucial. Ownership means embracing adaptability and being open to change. Continuously monitor market trends, customer needs, and industry shifts. When circumstances demand it, be willing to adjust your strategies and make bold decisions. Embrace flexibility and agility as key attributes that allow you to steer your business towards sustained growth and success.

Taking ownership of your decisions and actions in your business is a transformative mindset that fuels growth, resilience, and adaptability. By embracing ownership, you empower yourself to lead with confidence, make informed decisions, and navigate the challenges that come your way. Remember, ownership is not about controlling every outcome but about taking responsibility for the choices you make and learning from them.

As you embark on this journey of ownership, commit to a mindset of continuous learning, seeking guidance when needed, and embracing failures as stepping stones to success. Embrace the risks and responsibilities that come with entrepreneurship, knowing that they are essential elements of growth. Cultivate a strong company culture that values ownership and empowers your team members to take initiative and make decisions aligned with the business's vision.

In the ever-evolving business landscape, remain adaptable and flexible, ready to embrace change and seize new opportunities. Embrace innovation and a willingness to iterate your strategies to stay ahead of the curve. By taking ownership, you position your business for long-term success and create a legacy built on integrity, resilience, and achievement.

Remember, ownership is not a one-time event but a mindset and commitment that should permeate every aspect of your business. Embrace it wholeheartedly, and watch as your business thrives and flourishes under your inspired leadership. With ownership at the forefront, you have the power to shape your business's destiny and make a meaningful impact in the lives of your customers, employees, and stakeholders. Seize the opportunity and take ownership of your decisions and your business to unlock its true potential.

Taking ownership of your decisions and actions in your business is instrumental in building trust and credibility. When you demonstrate accountability and stand by the choices you make, you establish yourself as a reliable and trustworthy business leader. Customers, employees, and partners are more likely to have confidence in your business when they see that you take ownership of both successes and failures.

Communicate openly and transparently about the decisions you make, providing insights into the rationale behind them. When challenges arise, take responsibility, and openly address them with integrity and a commitment to finding solutions. By doing so, you foster an environment of trust and credibility, which strengthens your relationships and enhances your business's reputation.

Taking ownership extends beyond your own decisions; it involves empowering your team members to take ownership as well. Encourage a culture of accountability and provide your employees with the autonomy and authority to make decisions within their roles. Foster an environment where everyone feels a sense of ownership and responsibility for the success of the business. Recognize and celebrate instances where team members demonstrate ownership, and provide support and resources to help them succeed.

Ownership of decisions in your business requires a commitment to continuous improvement. Regularly evaluate the outcomes of your decisions and identify areas for growth and refinement. Embrace a mindset of constant learning, seeking feedback from customers, employees, and other stakeholders. Use the insights gained to make informed adjustments and optimize your strategies. By consistently striving for improvement, you ensure that your business stays relevant and resilient in a rapidly changing marketplace.

As a business leader, it is crucial to inspire and cultivate a culture of ownership within your organization. Lead by example, demonstrating ownership in your own decision-making processes and actions. Encourage and empower your employees to take initiative, think creatively, and take ownership of their work. Foster an environment where mistakes are viewed as learning opportunities, and accountability is embraced. By nurturing a culture of ownership, you create a dynamic and engaged team that is motivated to contribute to the success of the business.

Taking ownership of your decisions and actions in your business is a transformative mindset that propels growth, builds trust, and empowers your team. Embrace the responsibility that comes with entrepreneurship, learning from both successes and failures along the way. Foster a culture of ownership, where every member of your team feels empowered to contribute and take initiative. Continuously strive for improvement, adapt to change, and inspire others to embrace ownership. By doing so, you pave the way for long-term success, innovation, and fulfillment in your business journey. Embrace ownership, and watch your business flourish under your committed and visionary leadership.

Taking ownership of your decisions and business also requires developing resilience in the face of challenges. As a business owner, you will inevitably encounter obstacles and setbacks along the way. However, by taking ownership, you can approach these challenges with a proactive and solution-oriented mindset.

When faced with difficulties, resist the temptation to place blame on external factors. Instead, focus on what you can control and take responsibility for finding solutions. Embrace a resilient mindset that allows you to adapt, pivot, and persevere. Take the opportunity to learn from the challenges and use them as catalysts for growth and innovation.

Ownership of your decisions in business opens doors to innovation and creativity. By taking ownership, you empower yourself to think outside the box and explore new possibilities. Embrace a culture of innovation within your business, encouraging your team to contribute their ideas and perspectives. Embrace the entrepreneurial spirit and be willing to take calculated risks in pursuit of innovative solutions. By fostering a culture of ownership and creativity, you position your business to stay ahead of the competition and thrive in a rapidly evolving marketplace.

Taking ownership of your decisions and actions is a fundamental aspect of effective leadership. By assuming responsibility for the outcomes, you inspire confidence and trust in your leadership. Act as a role model for your team, demonstrating accountability, and showing them the importance of taking ownership in their own roles. Effective leadership based on ownership fosters a sense of purpose, motivation, and alignment within the organization.

To reinforce the importance of ownership, regularly review and reflect on the outcomes of your decisions. Assess the impact they have had on your business and identify any areas where adjustments or improvements can be made. Celebrate successes and acknowledge the lessons learned from any setbacks. By engaging in this ongoing process of review and reflection, you continually refine your decision-making skills and strengthen your ownership mindset.

Taking ownership of your decisions and business is a transformative approach that sets the stage for growth, resilience, and success. By embracing responsibility, you build trust, foster innovation, and inspire your team. Overcome challenges with resilience, embrace creativity, and embody effective leadership. Continually review and reflect on your decisions to learn and improve. By embracing ownership, you empower yourself and your business to reach new heights and achieve long-term success. Embrace this mindset and watch as your business flourishes and thrives in a competitive and ever-changing marketplace.

The Next Level

In the vast landscape of life, where possibilities stretch beyond the horizon, we find ourselves constantly yearning for progress and fulfillment. It is within this context that we must embrace the belief that there is always room for growth and expansion. Just as the universe expands ceaselessly, so too can our own potential and capacity to achieve greatness.

As human beings, we are born with an innate desire to explore, to push boundaries, and to evolve. We possess the remarkable ability to adapt, learn, and transform ourselves in the face of challenges and opportunities. Yet, at times, we may find ourselves trapped in self-imposed limitations or hindered by a fear of the unknown.

It is during these moments that we must remind ourselves of the vastness of our potential and the boundless opportunities that lie ahead.

The journey of growth and expansion begins with a mindset shift, an acknowledgment that we are not defined by our current circumstances or abilities. We have the power to shape our own destinies, to cultivate our strengths, and to acquire new skills and knowledge. It is essential to adopt a growth mindset, recognizing that every experience, whether positive or negative, serves as a stepping stone for our personal development.

Just as a seedling requires nurturing and nourishment to grow into a majestic tree, so too do we require the right environment and resources to flourish. Surrounding ourselves with like-minded individuals who inspire and challenge us, seeking out mentors and role models who have trodden the path we aspire to walk, and exposing ourselves to new ideas and perspectives are essential ingredients for our growth.

However, growth is not solely confined to our personal lives. It extends to our careers, relationships, and every facet of our existence. Professional growth involves continuously honing our skills, taking on new challenges, and embracing innovation in a rapidly evolving world. When we approach our work with an open mind and a willingness to learn, we create opportunities for advancement and the realization of our true potential.

Likewise, our relationships with others can be a source of growth and expansion. Each interaction provides an opportunity for understanding, empathy, and personal growth. By embracing diversity and actively seeking out connections with people from different backgrounds and cultures, we broaden our horizons and develop a more nuanced perspective of the world.

Relationships can act as catalysts for growth, challenging us to overcome our biases, expand our empathy, and foster deep connections.

It is important to remember that growth is not solely measured by external achievements or material possessions. True growth stems from within, from the cultivation of our values, passions, and personal well-being. Taking care of our physical and mental health, pursuing our passions, and nurturing our spiritual selves are all integral parts of the growth process. When we prioritize self-care and self-discovery, we create a solid foundation upon which growth can flourish.

As we navigate the ever-changing landscape of life, we must remember that growth and expansion are not destinations but rather ongoing journeys. The road may be winding, with unforeseen obstacles and detours, but it is through these challenges that we find our greatest opportunities for growth. Embrace the unknown, embrace the discomfort, and step outside of your comfort zone. It is in these moments of growth that you will discover the true extent of your capabilities.

Growth and expansion are inherent aspects of the human experience. They are the catalysts for personal and professional fulfillment, allowing us to reach new heights and make a lasting impact on the world around us. By adopting a growth mindset, nurturing our relationships, seeking out new experiences, and prioritizing our personal well-being, we can unlock the limitless potential that resides within each of us. Remember, there is always room for growth and expansion; it is up to us to seize the opportunity and embark on a transformative journey.

In the pursuit of growth and expansion, it is crucial to cultivate resilience and embrace failure as an essential part of the process. Each setback or disappointment is an opportunity to learn, adjust, and emerge stronger. Instead of viewing failure as a roadblock, see it as a stepping stone on the path to success. With each setback, you gain valuable insights, refine your approach, and develop the necessary skills to overcome future challenges.

ABOUT THE AUTHOR

Dr. Jeremy Lopez is Founder and President of Identity Network and Now Is Your Moment. Identity Network is one of the world's leading prophetic resource sites, offering books, teachings, and courses to a global audience. For more than thirty years, Dr. Lopez has been considered a pioneering voice within the field of the prophetic arts and his proven strategies for success coaching are now being implemented by various training groups and faith groups throughout the world. Dr. Lopez is the author of more than forty books, including his international bestselling books The Universe is at Your Command and Creating with Your Thoughts. Throughout his career, he has spoken prophetically into the lives of heads of business as well as heads of state. He has ministered to Governor Bob Riley of the State of Alabama, Prime Minister Benjamin Netanyahu, and Shimon Peres. Dr. Lopez continues to be a highly sought conference teacher and host, speaking on the topics of human potential and spirituality.

PROPHETIC READINGS

What is the Holy Spirit saying about your future? Find out by scheduling your personal prophecy with Dr. Jeremy Lopez today. To schedule your prophetic reading, contact the office of Identity Network at www.identitynetwork.net.

DREAM INTERPRETATION

Dreams are a gateway to Heavenly realms. What do your dreams say about your future and destiny? Find out with a personal dream interpretation from Dr. Jeremy Lopez. To schedule your own dream interpretation, contact the offices of Identity by visiting www.identitynetwork.net.